Key Stage Two Science Comprehensions

Short Stories to Aid Understanding

Mark Inder

Copyright © 2022 Mark Inder

The right of Mark Inder to be identified as the author of this work has been asserted by him in accordance with sections 77 and 78 of the Copyright, Designs and Patents Act 1988.

All rights reserved. No parts of this book may be reprinted or reproduced or utilised in any form or by any electronic, mechanical, or other means, now known or hereafter invented, including photocopying and recording, or any information storage or retrieval system, without permission in writing from the publishers.

British Library Cataloguing-in-Publication Data

A catalogue record for this book is available from the British Library

ISBN: 979-8-4256-4503-6

Typeset in Athelas

By PZAZ Publishing UK

ABOUT THE AUTHOR

Mark Inder is a secondary science teacher by trade but has spent eight years in the primary sector, helping to bring practical science to schools by training 2000+ teachers in over 400 UK primary schools, as well as developing schemes of work and writing, directing, presenting, and producing training videos.

In 2020, he founded the Primary Science Advisory Service – otherwise known as PZAZ – a company offering the first ever science function management system for primary schools. This system is used by over 2500 schools around the world.

He currently splits his time between London and Liverpool, and lives with one partner, one son, one cat and one giant African land snail.

ACKNOWLEDGEMENTS

I would like to thank Dan Sullivan who took me from ignominy and made me into something without even knowing it.

DEDICATION

For the people who have been with me since the beginning - my folks Charlie and Maureen as well as my brother Andy who came ever so slightly later.

TABLE OF CONTENTS

INTRODUCTION 15
HOW TO USE THIS BOOK 17
YEAR THREE 19
    Animals including Humans – Nutrition 20
        FEED YOUR HEALTH 20
    Animals including Humans – The Skeleton 22
        THE BROKEN ARM 22
    Animals including Humans – Muscles 24
        MARATHON RUNNER 24
    Rocks – An Introduction to Rocks 26
        GEOLOGY ROCKS! 26
    Rocks – Sedimentary and Metamorphic Rocks 28
        ROCK TYPES 28
    Rocks – Volcanic Rocks 30
        ROCKS FROM VOLCANOES 30
    Rocks – Fossils 33
        OLD BONES 33
    Rocks – Soils 36
        IT'S NOT JUST DIRT! 36
    Forces – Friction 38
        SLAM ON! 38
    Forces – Magnetism 41
        MAGNETIC METALS 41

- Light – Reflection 43
  - SNOW BLIND 43
- Light – Shadows 46
  - THE FAMOUS OXFORD SUNDIAL 46
- Plants – Roots 49
  - THE THIRSTY TREE 49
- Plants – Roots 51
  - PLANTS ARE SOLAR POWERED 51
- Plants – Stems 54
  - A TRUNK IS A STEM! 54
- Plants – Flowers 56
  - FLOWERS ARE NOT JUST FOR DECORATION 56
- Plants – Nutrients 58
  - PLANTS NEED FOOD TOO 58
- Plants – Light and Water 60
  - THE PLANT WITH NO LIGHT 60

YEAR FOUR 62
- Animals including Humans – The Digestive System 63
  - UNBALANCED DIET 63
- Animals including Humans – Teeth 66
  - A TRIP TO THE DENTIST 66
- Animals including Humans – Food Chains 69
  - WHO EATS WHO? 69
- Electricity – Circuits 71
  - THE UNLIT BULB 71
- Electricity – Conductors 73
  - METALS ARE CONDUCTORS 73

States of Matter – Solids 75
    PARTICLES 75
States of Matter – Liquids 78
    THE OIL SPILL 78
States of Matter – Gases 81
    THE ACCIDENT IN INDIA 81
States of Matter – Changes of State 83
    FREEZING AND MELTING 83
States of Matter – The Water Cycle 86
    WATER MOVES AROUND THE EARTH 86
Living Things and their Habitats – Classification 89
    HOW WE GROUP ANIMALS... 89
Living Things and their Habitats – Extinction 92
    PLATE TECTONICS 92
Sound – How Sounds are Made 95
    SOUND STARTS WITH VIBRATION 95
Sound – How Sounds Travel 97
    SOUND CAN GO THROUGH ANYTHING! 97
Sound – Pitch 99
    A NIGHT AT THE OPERA 99
Sound – Volume 102
    PROTECT YOUR EARS! 102
Sounds – Sound and Distance 104
    SOUNDS CAN TRAVEL FAR 104

YEAR FIVE 107

Forces – Gravity 108
    JUPITER WILL CRUSH YOU 108

- Forces – Friction 111
  - FRICTION PRODUCES HEAT 111
- Forces – Air Resistance 113
  - THE PARACHUTE JUMP 113
- Forces – Water Resistance 116
  - BOAT SHAPES 116
- Forces – Simple Machines 118
  - BICYCLE GEARS 118
- Properties and Changes of Materials – Burning 120
  - YOU NEED THREE THINGS FOR A FIRE 120
- Properties and Changes of Materials – Acid and Bicarbonate of Soda 122
  - HOW WE KNOW SOMETHING IS AN ACID 122
- Properties and Changes of Materials – Dissolving, Mixtures and Changes of State 125
  - SOLUTE + SOLVENT = SOLUTION 125
- Properties and Changes of Materials - Filtering 128
  - THE COFFEE SHOP 128
- Properties and Changes of Materials – Evaporation 131
  - TURNING LIQUID INTO GAS 131
- Properties and Changes of Materials – Hardness 133
  - A VISIT TO THE BLACKSMITH 133
- Properties and Changes of Materials – Transparency 136
  - SMART GLASS 136
- Properties and Changes of Materials – Electrical Conductors ... 138
  - CONDUCTORS FOR SAFETY 138

Space – the Solar System..140
    SPACE DOCUMENTARY..140

Space – The Earth and the Moon 143
    THE MOON ORBITS THE EARTH 143

Animals including Humans – The Human Life Cycle..................146
    THE RIDDLE 146

Living Things and their Habitats – Animal Life Cycles................ 147
    NOT ALL MAMMALS GIVE BIRTH 147

Living Things and their Habitats – Plant Reproduction 150
    HOW PLANTS PRODUCE OFFSPRING............................150

YEAR SIX... 152

Animals including Humans – The Heart and Circulatory System 153
    THE CHECK UP... 153

Animals including Humans – Diet 156
    AN UNBALANCED DIET 156

Animals including Humans – Exercise 158
    JOINING THE GYM 158

Animals including Humans – The Transport of Nutrients and Water 160
    WATER AND THE KIDNEYS....................................160

Electricity – Circuits.. 162
    CELLS AND BATTERIES 162

Light – Reflection 164
    A NIGHT TRIP ON A COUNTRY ROAD 164

Living Things and their Habitats - Microorganisms 167
    TINY LIVING THINGS WE CAN'T SEE 167

Living Things and their Habitats – Classification 169
  DON'T USE HABITATS TO CLASSIFY ANIMALS 169

Evolution and Inheritance - Adaptation 172
  THE GIRAFFE'S NECK 172

Evolution and Inheritance – Inheritance 175
  CHARACTERISTICS ARE PASSED ON 175

Evolution and Inheritance – Evolution 178
  THE ADVANTAGE OF ADAPTATION 178

INTRODUCTION

The ability to communicate is the most important life-skill an individual can possess. To a certain extent, our success in life depends on how well we can communicate with others. This enables us to beat the competition to get that job we desperately want or secure a contract that will ensure the future prosperity of businesses we create.

We could go on and on with examples of where communication is inextricably linked with success.

In education, there has been a huge focus on literacy (along with numeracy) for as long as anybody can remember. Written and spoken English is entwined with every area of the curriculum to give children these skills that will stay with them for the rest of their lives.

For science, the importance of literacy is paramount. It is central to a young person's success in the subject, as there are many technical terms that pupils need to use in context as they go through their learning journey. It is because of these technical terms is one reason that can make teaching and learning the subject of science difficult.

Using short stories is an excellent way to promote comprehension of a topic; particularly if pupils can relate the story to their own experiences. The contents of this book will help you convey the meanings behind much of the technical information that pupils need to learn. Each story has been written to engage children, and wherever possible, link to their own experiences, thus improving Science Capital.

Mark Inder

HOW TO USE THIS BOOK

Inside this book contains a short story for every science topic at Key Stage Two. They are designed to help teach the substantive knowledge pupils need, whilst at the same time allowing them to relate the events in many to their own experiences, and therefore make the teaching and learning of the subject matter easier.

The content is set out by year group in a similar manner to the national curriculum, but you may introduce the stories at any point in pupils' learning journey. Each story should take up no more than 15 minutes of your lessons, but they will no doubt promote much discussion. As ever, use your own judgement as to how long you need to spend on the stories.

The comprehensions have several questions that you could ask pupils, but these are not an exhaustive list, so please feel free to add your own or amend those given.

The content is set out in year group order in the same way as the National Curriculum, and you can use them to introduce a topic, assess pupil progress or even use to the stories to recall content previously taught.

Mark Inder

YEAR THREE

Key Stage Two Science Comprehensions

Animals including Humans – Nutrition

FEED YOUR HEALTH

Anita, the famous TV chef, was in the television studio filming her latest episode of 'Feed your Health': 'This dish is a real tasty, healthy treat,' she explained. 'The steamed Halibut will give you lots of protein, the brown rice contains lots of healthy carbohydrates and is low on unhealthy carbohydrates – and by that, I mean low in sugars.'

She looked at the camera and smiled. 'Then that beautiful broccoli stir-fried in rapeseed oil gives a real crunch to the dish as well as all the vitamin A, C and B you'll need and crucial minerals such as iron for healthy blood and calcium to keep those bones and teeth nice and strong, and the oil is rich in omega-3 fats so it's good for your ticker.

Finally, to round the dish off, the wilted spinach provides all that fibre to keep you regular and give you more vitamins and minerals.'

She paused for a moment before continuing. 'For you vegetarians and vegans, just replace the fish with 150g of red lentils, you'll still get the protein you need for growth and repair of your body's cells. Best of all, this dish only costs £2 per person to make. So, ditch the fried chicken and get cooking!'

Questions

1) What does your body use protein for?
2) What is a vegetarian?
3) What type of food is an unhealthy carbohydrate?
4) What mineral do you need for healthy blood?
5) Name a healthy fat.
6) What nutrient group is the main constituent of fish?

Answers

1) Growth and repair.
2) A human that eats only plants.
3) Sugar.
4) Iron.
5) Omega-3.
6) Protein.

Key Stage Two Science Comprehensions

Animals including Humans – The Skeleton

THE BROKEN ARM

Johnny and Amy were riding their bikes when Johnny hit a bump and fell off. They both heard a loud snap. 'I've broken my arm!' he cried. Sometime later, Johnny was in hospital with his mum getting treatment.

'Well Johnny,' reported Dr. Singh, 'we've just got your X-ray back, and you can see that you've broken your radius, which is the larger bone in your lower arm.' Although Johnny was in pain, he was very brave, and he loved riding his bike. 'When can I go biking with Amy again doctor?' The doctor thought for a moment. 'Well, usually you would be out of action for six weeks, but if you drink lots of milk and eat some cheese every day, you might heal faster.

'You see, dairy foods have lots of calcium in them, and calcium keeps your bones strong.' Johnny's eyes lit up: 'I love cheese and milk – I'll eat double what I do now!' The doctor laughed, 'I'm sure you will, but you will need to come back in a month so I can see how you're healing.'

Questions

1) What is the name of the bone that Johnny broke?
2) Where is the Johnny's broken bone?
3) What is an X-ray for?
4) What mineral makes bones strong?
5) What foods are rich in this mineral?

Answers

1) The radius.
2) His arm.
3) To see inside the body.
4) Calcium.
5) Dairy foods.

Key Stage Two Science Comprehensions

Animals including Humans – Muscles

MARATHON RUNNER

Ahmed was watching the Olympic Marathon Race with his older sister, Khadija who was studying sports science at university. 'Look at Mo Farah.' said Ahmed, 'his legs are really big, but his arms are skinny – I wonder why that is?' Khadija thought for a moment, 'Oh that's easy,' she boasted, 'he has to run fast for 26 miles, and it will take him about 2 hours, so the muscles in his legs must be big, particularly his thigh muscle, which has the posh name Quadriceps Femoris.

'The thing is, he doesn't really need big arms to power his body, so they're thin because he doesn't exercise them so much.' 'Ah I get it,' thought Ahmed, 'if he did loads of weights to exercise his arms, they would get bigger, and he wouldn't be able to run so fast because he would be heavier?' 'You got it, and don't forget his hamstring muscles behind his thigh are working hard too to bend his leg. In fact, they work together with the Quad muscle to move the legs' replied Khadija.

'Yeeesssss!' exclaimed Ahmed, who didn't seem to be listening anymore, 'He's won the gold medal!'

Questions

1) Where on your body is the Quadriceps muscle?
2) What happens to muscles when you exercise them?
3) What is the name of the 2 muscles in your leg that work together?
4) What movement do your legs make when you run?
5) What joints do you think are involved in bending the legs and the arms?

Answers

1) The thigh.
2) The grow larger and stronger.
3) Quadriceps Femoris and hamstrings.
4) They bend and then straighten.
5) The knee and the elbow joints.

Key Stage Two Science Comprehensions

Rocks – An Introduction to Rocks

GEOLOGY ROCKS!

Oscar was reading a book about rocks. It said: 'The Study of Rocks is called Geology. There are many different rocks, but they all fall into one of 3 categories: sedimentary, metamorphic, and igneous. Each has its own characteristics that allow geologists to classify them.

Igneous rocks are formed from molten rock which then cools and solidifies. As we know, volcanoes produce a lot of molten rock which we call lava. Examples of igneous rocks are granite and pumice.

Metamorphic rocks such as slate and marble form when sedimentary or igneous rocks are subjected to high temperatures and pressure deep in the Earth.

Finally, sedimentary rocks are formed from small pieces of broken-down rock that clump together and over time get squashed together to form layered rock. Limestone, Sandstone and Chalk are examples. Even coal is a sedimentary rock!

Questions

1) What are the 3 types of rock?
2) What happens to molten rock for it to make an igneous rock?
3) Name 2 metamorphic rocks.
4) How is sedimentary rock formed?
5) What is a geologist and what do they do?

Answers

1) Igneous, Metamorphic and Sedimentary.
2) It cools and solidifies.
3) Slate and marble.
4) Small rocks clump together and then are squashed together.
5) Geologists study rocks

Key Stage Two Science Comprehensions

Rocks – Sedimentary and Metamorphic Rocks

ROCK TYPES

Yasmina walked into the Geology section of the museum. A voice immediately started speaking overhead: 'Sedimentary Rocks are rocks that are formed from the broken pieces of other rocks that become joined together. These pieces are usually quite small, and usually they get carried by rivers either out to sea, or even lakes.

'When these rock pieces reach these larger bodies of water, the rock pieces fall to the bottom. This is called deposition. Then, over time these small pieces get covered in other pieces of rock, so layers called sediments begin to form. All this weight begins to squash the bits below it together. Scientists call this compaction.'

The voice paused for a second. 'The sediments lose all the water because of this squeezing just like when you wring out a dish cloth, and at this point, all the original little pieces of rock are stuck together. This final stage is named cementation. You now have your sedimentary rock, and its formation takes millions of years. The sandstone, mudstone, and limestone pieces in the cabinet on your left were all formed by this process.'

Questions

1) What are sedimentary rocks formed from?
2) What does deposition mean?
3) What does compaction mean?
4) What does cementation mean?

Answers

1) Small pieces of rock
2) Small pieces of rock falling to the bottom of water.
3) When small pieces of rock get squashed together.
4) The point where all the small pieces of rock are stuck together.

Key Stage Two Science Comprehensions

Rocks – Volcanic Rocks

ROCKS FROM VOLCANOES

Pedro and his dad were watching a documentary on volcanic eruptions, presented by world famous geologist Dr. Claudia Alexander who was in Naples, Italy standing on the smoking volcano Vesuvius. 'Igneous rocks are made when molten rock cools and solidifies. This can happen both inside and outside a volcano,' she said, 'and this is important because the molten rock cools at different rates, forming different rocks. The cooling rate affects how big the crystals of mineral are in the rock formed.

'For example, molten rock inside the volcano or even deep below the Earth's surface doesn't cool very quickly, and this allows large crystals inside the rock to be made. We call these intrinsic igneous rocks. It's easy to remember – intrinsic starts with 'in', and they are inside which also starts with 'in' – easy huh?' She continued, 'examples of intrinsic igneous rock are granite and gabbro.'

She looked down at the ground and picked up a rock which she showed to the camera. 'This is pumice, which formed outside the volcano – an extrinsic igneous rock. When it erupted and all the lava landed here, it cooled really quickly, so the crystals in the rock are small.

'Sometimes the rocks cool so quickly that they form volcanic glass!' She looked around again. 'Ah here is some! Obsidian – black volcanic glass that forms outside the volcano, so another extrinsic igneous rock.'

Questions

1) How are igneous rocks made?
2) What does the cooling rate affect?
3) Are large or small crystals made when cooling occurs quickly?
4) Where is an intrinsic igneous rock made?
5) Give 2 examples of extrinsic igneous rock.

Answers

1) When molten rock cools.
2) How big the crystals are in the rock.
3) Small crystals are formed.
4) Inside a volcano.
5) Pumice and Obsidian.

Mark Inder

Rocks – Fossils

OLD BONES

Tariq and Leona were on a school visit to the museum. 'And here,' the guide said proudly, 'is Lizzie, our T-Rex skeleton.' Tariq put his hand up, 'Shouldn't those bones be white?'

'They're not actually bones,' answered the guide. 'This magnificent specimen is a fossil. That is: the remains of a plant or animal that had become trapped in rock and eventually, every part of the plant or animal becomes petrified, which means turned to stone.'

'How long does it take to turn into a fossil?' asked Leona. 'It depends on what's being fossilised,' replied the guide, 'some things may only take a thousand years, but bigger things can take tens of thousands of years to become fossils.'

'How does it happen in the first place?' enquired Tariq. The guide thought for a moment. 'Let's say you have a Carnotaurus that's about to die. It dies next to a river and falls in and sinks to the bottom. Over time, sand and mud and other sediments cover it to the point that all that matter piled on top of the animal starts to get heavy so there is a lot of pressure, and all that stuff gets compacted together over time to form rock, and the animal itself changes too.

'As I've already said, this process of fossilisation takes a long time.' The guide pointed towards the T-Rex. 'Lizzie here was discovered 20 years ago by a type of scientist called a palaeontologist, who dug her up and brought her to us. She originally lived 66 million years ago.'

Questions

1) What is a fossil?
2) How long can fossilisation take?
3) What piles on top of the animal or plant for fossilisation to take place?
4) Who digs up fossils?

Answers

1) The remains of a plant or animal that has become trapped in rock and turned to stone.
2) It can take over 10,000 years.
3) Mud and sand.
4) Palaeontologists.

Key Stage Two Science Comprehensions

Rocks – Soils

IT'S NOT JUST DIRT!

Oscar was talking to the school gardener. 'Why do you do that job when you can get so dirty?' The gardener smiled as he continued to shovel soil, 'I do it because I can get dirty! Seriously though, to me, soil is really interesting.' 'Interesting?' enquired Oscar, 'it's just dirt.' 'No no no,' replied the gardener seriously, 'it's much more than that. 50% of it is made up of air and water, with the rest being minerals and organic matter like worms and dead leaves.

'In just one gram, there could be 7000 different types of bacteria. In one year, worms found in an area the size of half a football pitch can eat 15 tonnes of soil because there are so many minerals in there that they need. Plants love those same minerals!'

He brightened as he spoke. 'Do you know there are a few types of soil: sandy, silty, clay, peaty and saline. They all have different properties. For example, sandy soil drains water much better than clay, and this can make a difference when you're deciding what crops you should grow.' 'Wow!' exclaimed Oscar, 'dirt is more complicated than I thought!'

Questions

1) What percentage of soil is made up by organic matter?
2) How many types of soil are there?
3) What do worms do with soil? Why do they do this?
4) Name one property of soil.

Answers

1) 50%
2) At least 5.
3) The eat the soil as they need the minerals.
4) It can drain water.

Key Stage Two Science Comprehensions

Forces – Friction

SLAM ON!

Dad and I were driving to the shops. Suddenly, another car pulled out in front of us, and Dad had to slam on the brakes. The car came to a screeching halt quite quickly. Dad honked the horn angrily.

'Why does the car stop when you press the brake pedal Dad?' I enquired. 'Well son, it's the same as when you brake on your bike. When you want to slow down or stop, you squeeze the lever on the handlebars which causes a brake pad to touch the wheel making it harder for the wheel to turn, so your bike slows down and eventually stops. You see, when two surfaces touch each other, there is a force that acts on them called friction. Friction acts to slow objects down or even stop them from moving. It's pretty useful as we've just seen, without it we would have crashed into that other car!'

I thought for a moment. 'So, without the brake pad, there is no friction?' 'Oh no,' he replied, 'the wheels are touching the road remember? The road surface must be rough to stop cars sliding everywhere, which is what happens when it rains. The water acts as a lubricant, which reduces the amount of friction by making the road smoother.'

He thought for a moment. 'If you're on your bike and you need to stop quickly, you have to pull that brake lever more forcefully. That way, the brake pad and the tyre are pressed together harder and this produces more friction, so you stop quicker.'

Questions

1) What is the force called that slows objects down?
2) How does it slow objects down?
3) Which slows objects down more quickly, rough or smooth objects?
4) What do lubricants do?
5) What happens to two objects that are pressed together more forcefully?

Answers

1) Friction.
2) When 2 surfaces come into contact with each other they slow the movement.
3) Rough objects show more friction.
4) They reduce the amount of friction.
5) There is more friction.

Mark Inder

Forces – Magnetism

MAGNETIC METALS

Olivia was doing some research on magnetism whilst her mum was watching the TV. 'Cool!' she exclaimed, 'Mum, did you know that the Earth is a giant magnet?' 'That's nice,' said mum distractedly.

'Because the centre of the Earth – the core - is made mainly of 2 metals, nickel and iron. Just like every other magnet, there is an invisible field around the Earth called the magnetic field. This is the thing that makes the Northern Lights!

'The further out from the magnet, the weaker its magnetic field gets. It says here that cobalt is another metal that is magnetic, but metals such as copper and aluminium won't be attracted to a magnet, and non-metals aren't attracted to them at all.'

'Oh, I remember some of that from school,' remarked mum, 'Magnets have 2 poles, and when the same poles are facing each other, they are repelled, meaning they move away from each other, and when opposite poles are together, they're attracted. Different magnets have different strengths too.' She turned back to the TV. 'Mum!' said Olivia with a hint of exasperation in her voice, 'I wanted to find that out for myself!'

Questions

1) What are all magnets surrounded by?
2) What happens to the magnetic field as it gets further away from the magnet?
3) What types of materials are not attracted to magnets?
4) Name 5 metals.
5) What happens when like poles are facing each other?

Answers

1) A magnetic field.
2) It gets weaker.
3) Non-metals.
4) Iron, cobalt, nickel, aluminium, magnesium (anything on the left-hand side of the Periodic table!)
5) They repel.

Mark Inder

Light – Reflection

<u>SNOW BLIND</u>

Ruby and Alex were on a school skiing trip to Italy, and they were having a safety briefing. 'We'll come on to the rules of the slopes in a moment,' the instructor said, 'but first, we need to talk about these.' she grabbed a set of ski goggles off a table. They had a single gold lens that covered both eyes.

The instructor put them on, and Ruby and Alex could see that the goggles fit snuggly to her cheeks and forehead. 'You must have these on at all times when you're on the slopes, and you have to fit them properly so there are no gaps between the goggles and your skin. It may not seem like it, but the sunlight is very dangerous up here. The snow acts like a giant mirror, and all that light is reflected off the snow. Prolonged exposure to this reflected light will make you snow blind. That would certainly ruin your holiday for at least 3 days.'

'Snow blind!' exclaimed Ruby, 'I've never heard of it. What happens?' The instructor was serious as she answered. 'Think of it as sunburn for the inside of your eye. Your eyes can't protect themselves from the dangerous ultraviolet radiation that comes from the Sun, so you have to wear these as they block the harmful light.' She pointed to her goggles.

'If you don't, you'll be in severe pain for 3 days where you won't be able to see because your eyes are completely covered and as we all know, without light entering your eyes you can't see.

'We'd have to lock you in a room and block all the light from entering so it will be in total darkness – a completely unpleasant experience for anybody foolish enough to not wear their goggles.' Her voice took on a tone of command. 'Do you all understand what I've just told you?' Thirty heads nodded vigorously. 'Good!' she smiled, 'now on to the fun stuff!'

Questions

1) What happens to light that hits a mirror?
2) What type of radiation from the Sun can be dangerous?
3) What happens to your sight if there's no light to enter your eyes?
4) What is darkness?
5) How can you protect your eyes from the Sun's harmful rays?

Answers

1) It's reflected.
2) Ultraviolet.
3) You cannot see.
4) The absence of light.
5) Wear sunglasses that block harmful radiation.

Key Stage Two Science Comprehensions

Light – Shadows

THE FAMOUS OXFORD SUNDIAL

Lenny and his sister Gemma were sightseeing in Oxford. They were visiting Corpus Christi college, where there was a sundial that had stood there since 1581.

'Although this is old,' said their Tour Guide, 'it's by no means the oldest in the world. There is one in Egypt -in the Valley of the Kings - that dates to 1500 BC. Apparently, they used it to monitor working hours!' He finished with a laugh.

'Sir, how can this thing tell the time when it's just a tall, thin piece of concrete with some fancy decorations on it?' interrupted Gemma. Mum looked at her sternly for being so rude. The man turned to her with a gleam in his eye.

'Well, we know that some things don't let light through them, and we describe these as 'opaque objects.'' He glanced up at the column. 'When sunlight hits the column, the light is blocked so we see a dark shape on the opposite side of the column – this is the shadow. Notice it's basically the same shape as the column?'

Gemma sniffed her nose rudely. 'I understand that, but how can it tell time?' Dad was about to shout at her, but the tour guide shook his head and raised his hand to suggest all was well. He smiled again.

'It's just past lunchtime now, and because the Sun is directly overhead, the shadow is shorter than it is when sunlight first hits the column early in the morning, where there is a smaller angle between the light source – the Sun – and the sun dial. The shadow will start to get longer again as the Sun heads to the horizon. You see, the shadow moves around the column just like the hands on a clock. So, we can tell the time by the position of the shadow.' 'That is clever!' admitted Gemma.

Questions

1) How is a shadow formed?
2) What do opaque objects do to light?
3) What shape are shadows?
4) How could you make a shadow longer?
5) Give an example of a light source.

Answers

1) When light hits an opaque object, the light cannot pass through and so a dark area is produced.
2) They block it.
3) The same shape as the object that blocks the light.
4) The angle between the light source and the object is lowered.
5) The sun, lamp etc.

Mark Inder

Plants – Roots

THE THIRSTY TREE

'Why doesn't the wind blow that giant tree over?' asked James with awe, who was on holiday in California with his family. They were in a forest of Sequoia trees and looking at one that was over 300 feet tall. Shawna, their forest guide turned to him to answer.

'Can you believe the roots go down to only 20 feet? What keeps these plants upright is how wide their root system's spread,' she continued, 'and this one's root system is estimated to be the same area as one and a half football pitches.' James's family all uttered 'Wow!' at the same time.

Shawna smiled at their reaction, 'The roots need to be spread that wide so the tree can take all the minerals it needs from the soil. Not only that, but this tree alone can also take up 4500 litres of water a day through these roots, although it needs to be a hot day for that, and today it's hot!' They all gasped in wonder and turned their attention back to the tree.

Questions

1) What two things does the tree get from the soil?
2) How do these things get into the tree?
3) What environmental factor might affect how quickly these things are taken up by the tree?
4) What other function do the roots of the tree have?
5) What is the network of roots called?

Answers

1) Water and minerals.
2) Through the roots.
3) The temperature of the environment.
4) They provide stability.
5) The root system.

Plants – Roots

PLANTS ARE SOLAR POWERED

Sammy and Anvi were attending a lecture on plants at the Royal Institute. 'Leaves are one of the most remarkable parts of any living thing in the world,' the lecturer said, 'they can convert sunlight, carbon dioxide from the air and water from the ground into glucose – a high energy sugar. This process is called photosynthesis. The plant then strings this glucose together to produce starch, which is itself stored in the leaf.'

Anvi raised her hands. 'But plants don't eat!' she exclaimed. 'That's not quite true,' Dr. Green replied, 'but the difference between them and us is that they make their own food whereas we and other animals can't. The top of the leaf is the part that makes most of the food, the bottom has thousands of microscopic holes in it called stomata. They allow carbon dioxide from the air in, and oxygen which is also made by photosynthesis out. They also help regulate how much water the plant keeps by opening and closing depending on the conditions. Leaves come in all shapes on sizes depending on the species of plant and the habitat in which they live.'

Questions

1) What functions do leaves have?
2) What happens when the plant strings glucose together?
3) What happens to the starch?
4) Where are stomata found?
5) What do stomata do to regulate the amount of water in a plant?

Answers

1) They convert sunlight, carbon dioxide and water into food.
2) It becomes starch.
3) It is stored mainly in the leaf.
4) On the underside of the leaf.
5) They open and close.

Key Stage Two Science Comprehensions

Plants – Stems

A TRUNK IS A STEM!

Ryan was talking to his biology teacher, who was a qualified botanist. 'What's the point of the stem? Why can't a plant just get water from the roots which would be attached to the leaves?' he enquired. Mr. Malaka stroked his chin in thought before answering.

'The stem – which all plants have - is crucial in a plant,' his teacher explained, 'they provide a place where the leaves are in the best position to photosynthesise efficiently, they store many of the nutrients the plant needs to stay healthy and of course, they provide support.'

'Wait a minute sir, you said all plants have them, but trees have trunks, don't they? And surely a cactus doesn't have a stem?' 'A trunk is a stem,' laughed Mr. Malaka, 'it's just hard compared to other stems, and the part where the spikes grow on a cactus is the stem. They come in all shapes and sizes.

'Remember, just like any living thing, they are adapted to their environment. In any case, the stem's most important job is to get water to the leaves. There are tubes in the stem called xylems that do this. Scientists call this process transpiration,' Ryan thought for a moment, 'Okay sir you've convinced me, stems are important!' declared Ryan.

Questions

1) What is the process of transporting water through a plant called?
2) What are the tubes inside the stem that transport water called?
3) Where does the water finish its journey inside the plant?
4) What other thing is transported in these tubes?
5) What else does the stem do for the plant?

Answers

1) Transpiration.
2) Xylems.
3) At the leaves.
4) Minerals.
5) It stores nutrients.

Plants – Flowers

FLOWERS ARE NOT JUST FOR DECORATION

The aptly named Professor Flowers, the world-famous expert on prehistoric plants, was visiting school to give an assembly. 'Flowering plants first appeared in the Jurassic Period 160 million years ago, and this marked a time when the number of species of insects literally exploded.'

He was positively bouncing around the stage with enthusiasm. 'As we know, many flowering plants rely on insects to spread their pollen to other plants. Once this pollination takes place, the pollen grain, which is produced by the male part of the plant called the anther, sits on the female part, the stigma.'

He paused to take a breath. 'The stigma sits on top of a tube called the style which the pollen travels down all the way to the ovary to meet an egg, or as we boffins call it, the ovum, and they fuse together. This merging of the pollen and ovum is called fertilisation, and it results in a seed being formed.'

The Professor was now hopping excitedly. 'But the story doesn't end there, the seeds need to be dispersed so they can grow into new plant. The plant uses water, wind and animals to do this. Some plants even use explosions to disperse their seed!' He ended breathlessly.

Questions

1) What type of living thing was the pollinator in this story?
2) What part of the plant produces pollen?
3) Where does the pollen sit once pollination happens?
4) How is a seed formed?
5) What ways can seeds be dispersed?

Answers

1) Insect.
2) Anther.
3) Stigma.
4) The pollen fuses with the ovum.
5) Wind, Animal, Water, Explosion.

Key Stage Two Science Comprehensions

Plants – Nutrients

PLANTS NEED FOOD TOO

Libby and Anya were researching plant nutrients on the internet. They had to make a PowerPoint presentation for homework. 'Libby, look at this.' Anya said, 'It says here that plants have to have certain nutrients to grow and remain healthy, and those that don't get all they need have slower growth rates.'

'What does growth rate mean?' asked Libby. 'Hmm let me see….' Anya paused, 'Ah here it is. Growth rate is the growth length over time, and it says here that sunflowers have a growth rate of 15cm per week!

'Cool, that's why they're so tall!' Anya smiled, 'But I've found something else. It says here that plants use calcium to help them fight off diseases, and they also need magnesium, nitrogen, phosphorous, potassium, and sulphur. There are a few others too.

'Usually, the plant gets all these nutrients from the soil, but sometimes the soil doesn't have too many of these minerals, so some plants catch flies that gives them all the nutrients they need!' 'Ooh I'd love to see that!' exclaimed Libby. 'But I think we've got enough to do our homework now, so let's go!'

Questions

1) What are the main minerals plants need?
2) What happens if a plant doesn't get enough pf these minerals?
3) What do some plants do that grow in soil that is low in minerals?
4) What is growth rate?

Answers

1) Calcium, magnesium, nitrogen, phosphorous, potassium, and sulphur.
2) They can get diseases.
3) They can catch insects.
4) The amount of growth over time, for example centimetres per week.

Key Stage Two Science Comprehensions

Plants – Light and Water

THE PLANT WITH NO LIGHT

Mum and I had just returned from holiday, 'Oh look at that,' she said sadly, 'my spider plant has died.' I looked over to her. 'What do you expect?' I answered, 'We've been away for a month, and you insisted on pulling the blackout blind down while we were away, so it hasn't been getting any light. Without sunlight, the plant can't make its own food – it's called photosynthesis.'

She smiled at me, 'I'm glad you've been paying attention in class, what else have you learned?' she challenged. 'Well, it probably could get the carbon dioxide it needs from the air, but you didn't want Mrs. Hubbins next door to have a key, so the plant didn't get watered for a month - a plant can't photosynthesize without water either!' I replied.

Questions

1) What is the process of a plant making its own food called?
2) What 3 things do plants need to photosynthesise?
3) Where do plants get carbon dioxide from

Answers

1) Photosynthesis.
2) Carbon dioxide, water, sunlight.
3) The air.

YEAR FOUR

Animals including Humans – The Digestive System

UNBALANCED DIET

I was feeling a bit sick because I hadn't been to the toilet for four days, so I was in the doctors with my Mum.

'So, Liam,' the doctor asked, 'What have you been eating?' Before I could reply, Mum spoke. 'He read that if you only eat meat, you'll become super-strong, so he hasn't had any fruit, vegetables or cereal for nearly a week.'

She continued apologetically,' He's literally only eaten chicken, pork and beef in that time doctor.' The doctor raised an eyebrow.

'That's why you haven't been to the toilet Liam. You see, when you eat protein alone, it can stop the food moving through your digestive system properly. You need lots of fibre in your diet. When food leaves your stomach, it goes into a long tube called your intestine. The first part is the small intestine and then it becomes the large intestine.

'The food needs to move smoothly through your intestines so you can get all the nutrients your body needs – Digestion is the process where our bodies break down food into the nutrients we need to stay healthy.

'Anyway, eventually digestion just leaves what your body doesn't need – what you call poo – if you don't regularly get rid of this waste from your body through the anus, it will build up in your rectum and that's why you're feeling a bit sick. You need to make sure you get lots of fibre from what you eat and that means lots of cereal, fruit and vegetables. Okay?'

'Yes doctor.' I replied sheepishly. 'Good,' the doctor nodded, satisfied. 'Another thing. Make sure you chew your food properly as well. You might not know this, but digestion starts in your mouth. If you make your food as small as possible, it will be easier to swallow it. When you do swallow it, it goes down another tube called the oesophagus and that leads to our stomach.'

'You will, won't you Liam?' Mum said in a tone that I knew not to argue with. 'I'll make sure he will doctor,' promised Mum, 'and thank you!'

Questions

1) What substance makes your food move through your digestive system smoothly?
2) What foods can you eat to get enough this substance?
3) What is the name of the tube that food goes into after it has been in the stomach?
4) What is digestion?
5) Where does digestion start?
6) Where does all the waste leave the body?

Answers

1) Fibre.
2) Cereal, fruit and vegetables.
3) Small intestine.
4) The breakdown of food into the nutrients the body needs.
5) In the mouth.
6) The anus.

Key Stage Two Science Comprehensions

Animals including Humans – Teeth

A TRIP TO THE DENTIST

Izzy was worried she was going to lose her teeth because she thought that one was going black, so she was at the dentist with her Dad.

'I don't eat too many sweets I promise.' She claimed to Dr. Roberts. 'Well Izzie, I have some good news,' the dentist said, 'there is no sign of tooth decay here, which is what would happen if you ate too much sugary food and then not brush your teeth regularly.'

Izzy thought for a moment before replying. 'I brush my teeth when I get up every day.' Dr Roberts looked concerned. 'You need to brush before you sleep as well, because that gets rid of all the harmful bacteria on your teeth. The bacteria 'eats' sugar that's left on your teeth and then produces acid that causes the decay, and we don't want that.

'Make sure you spend enough time on all your teeth too,' advised the dentist, 'The ones at the top and bottom in the middle are called the incisors, which cut the food you eat, then next to your incisors are the canines, which tear the food, and then you have wider, flatter teeth called the premolars. The biggest teeth are at the back of your mouth are called molars.

'Both molars and premolars are good for crushing food as they have the same shape. If you lose any tooth, it'll be more difficult to eat your food.' 'Yes Dr. Roberts' promised Izzy.

Questions

1) What happens if you eat too much sugary food and then don't brush your teeth regularly?
2) How many times a day should you brush your teeth?
3) What does brushing your teeth do?
4) Which types of tooth crushes food?
5) What is the name of the tooth that is next to the incisors?

Answers

1) It can lead to tooth decay.
2) At least twice and preferably after meals.
3) Brushing removes the bacteria that feed on sugar.
4) Molars and pre-molars.

Mark Inder

Animals including Humans – Food Chains

WHO EATS WHO?

Lilah was watching a wildlife documentary on the Arctic at home with her family. The presenter had flecks of ice in his beard as he was talking about polar bears.

'In this habitat, the polar bear is the apex predator so it's at the top of the food chain. It mainly hunts ringed seals, which are easy prey as they gather in large numbers on the ice, where they spend so much time. The seals themselves feed on the plentiful cod which spawns in the Arctic waters around the ice sheet. The waters around here are rich in plankton, which the cod eat. The plankton themselves then feed on invisible aquatic plants called algae.

'Plants are always described as producers. When we come back, we will talk about how this food chain is threatened by the activities of mankind.'

Questions

1) How do we describe an animal at the top of the food chain?
2) What animals in the text are prey?
3) How do we always describe plants?

Answers

1) An apex predator.
2) Ringed seals, cod and plankton.
3) Producers.

Mark Inder

Electricity – Circuits

THE UNLIT BULB

'Miss! I can't get the bulb to work.' Andy and I were working together trying to build a circuit. Miss came over to us and looked at what we'd done.

'You haven't connected the lead to the cell,' explained Miss, 'How can the electricity get around the circuit to the bulb if your circuit is not connected?' I nudged Andy with my elbow. 'See I told you - I told him miss! The power can't jump across gaps in the circuit to power the components.'

Andy looked puzzled. 'What's a component?' Miss shook her head in exasperation. 'Explain it to him Chris. He clearly wasn't listening at the beginning of the lesson.'

I coughed before answering. 'A component is an item in a circuit that carries out some kind of function such as a bulb, which lights up, or a buzzer, which makes a noise. Components have their own special symbols so can draw proper circuit diagrams.'

'Very good. 10 points to Oak. Remember you need to add a switch into that circuit so you can open or close the circuit, thereby turn the components off and on. I'll be back to check on you two in 5 minutes.' Miss smiled and left. 'You get all the luck,' muttered Andy. 'I wasn't staring out the window when she told us.' I replied with a smug tone.

Questions

1) What is a component?
2) What can stop components from working in a circuit?
3) What do you need to know before you draw a circuit diagram?
4) How does a switch work?

Answers

1) An item in a circuit that carries out a certain function.
2) The circuit being open.
3) The circuit symbols.
4) It controls the flow of current in a circuit by opening and closing.

Mark Inder

Electricity – Conductors

METALS ARE CONDUCTORS

A man called Mr Robot was visiting our school. His job was to make the robots that make cars, and he was explaining to us how he did that. 'You need to have a good knowledge of how to build circuits to make a robot,' he explained, 'and that starts with materials called conductors. Conductors are substances that allow electricity to pass through them. Metals are good conductors of electricity.

'Materials that don't allow electricity to pass through them all tend to be non-metals like plastic, and we call those materials insulators.

He held up a finger. 'But there is one exception. Graphite is a type of carbon which is a non-metal, and it's a good conductor. Do you know that the inside bit of your pencil is graphite?

'Anyway, it may sound like insulators are useless when building circuits, but they are really important in safety because they will stop anyone from being electrocuted, and they are useful in devices like alarms as they stop the alarm from sounding all the time. Any questions so far?' A hundred hands shot in the air.

Questions

1) What is a material that allows electricity to pass through it called?
2) What types of material conduct electricity well?
3) What does an insulator do?
4) Which non-metal makes a good conductor?
5) Why are insulators important?

Answers

1) A conductor.
2) Metals.
3) It stops the flow of electrical current.
4) Graphite.
5) For safety.

Mark Inder

States of Matter – Solids

PARTICLES

Rosie was trying to do an essay entitled 'What is a state of matter?' – she was struggling to put words on paper so she thought she would call her big sister Marianne who was a materials scientist. She spent a minute or two explaining the problem.

'Well,' her sister said, 'you need to start with particles. Particles are the smallest part of a substance. Imagine you have a wall; the smallest particle of a wall is a brick. Imagine a beach, the smallest particle is a grain of sand.'

'I get that,' Rosie said testily, 'but I don't see how it helps me do this essay!' 'Don't get frustrated and let me finish.' Her sister ordered. 'You see, everything is made of particles – us, the stars, air, computer games, everything! Now, how tightly the particles are packed together depends on the state of matter of the substance.

'All solids have tightly packed particles. Imagine 25 balls packed together 5 across and 5 down. The balls are all touching each other. This is what particle diagrams for solids look like.'

'I see,' said Rosie thoughtfully, 'but what if it's a different solid?' 'Doesn't matter,' replied Marianne, 'the particles are all packed essentially in the same way. If you can draw one, you can draw them all!

'Liquid particle diagrams look kind of the same as solids, but there are some gaps between the particles, and liquids flow because the particles move into these gaps. Finally, when you're drawing gases, just have a load of separate particles on your diagram. It's like this because the particles in a gas have the most energy and are free to move anywhere.'

Questions

1) What is a particle?
2) Give an example of a particle?
3) How do the particles in a solid look?
4) How do liquids flow?
5) Which state of matter's particles have the most energy?

Answers

1) The smallest part of a substance.
2) An atom, or a molecule.
3) Tightly packed together.
4) There are gaps between the particles that particles can move into.
5) Gas.

Key Stage Two Science Comprehensions

States of Matter – Liquids

THE OIL SPILL

'Look at that Dad!' I shouted. The news was on, an oil tanker had crashed into some rocks in the Gulf of Mexico, and oil was spilling out of the tanker and had spread as far as the eye could see. There were sad pictures of birds covered in oil being treated.

'Yes son, an oil spill has terrible consequences for the environment,' said Dad, sadly. 'Why does the oil sit on top of the water Dad?' I asked. 'Well, he said, 'different liquids are denser than others. Density is the amount of mass of something in a certain space.

'In this case, oil is less dense than salt-water, so the oil sits on top. To clean the sea, they can scoop up the oil from the surface of the water. If the oil was denser, it would sink to the bottom of the sea, which would make clean up much more difficult.'

'I never thought about that,' I said, 'so if I had a load of honey – which is a liquid – it would sink to the bottom of the water?' 'Well honey is quite viscous, that is to say thick, but do you know I don't know the answer to that,' said Dad thoughtfully. 'Shall we find out? We've got honey and salt in the cupboard. Let's do an experiment!' 'Let's go!' I said excitedly.

Key Stage Two Science Comprehensions

Questions

1) What does density mean?
2) Why does oil sit on top of the water?
3) If you threw a rock into a river, why would it sink?
4) When you open a can of soda, you hear the hiss of a gas escaping from the liquid. Why?
5) What is the scientific term for the property of thickness of liquids?

Answers

1) The amount of mass in a certain space.
2) It is less dense than water.
3) It is denser than water.
4) The gas is less dense than the liquid so it leaves the can.
5) Viscosity.

Mark Inder

States of Matter – Gases

THE ACCIDENT IN INDIA

In 1984, the worst industrial accident occurred in human history. It occurred at a chemical plant owned by Union Carbide in Bhopal, India, where methyl isocyanate (MIC) gas escaped.

Over 500,000 people were exposed to this highly toxic gas, with 3,787 people killed by its effects. It is estimated that another 16,000 have died from the effects of the gas release. Effects included coughing, vomiting, severe eye irritation and breathlessness.

Originally, the MIC was stored as a liquid in storage tanks, but when one of the tanks became damaged, the liquid evaporated to produce the gas which spread quickly by moving through the air. Gas particles are more difficult to control than solids or liquids because they are free to move anywhere.

Questions

1) What was the name of the gas that caused problems?
2) Why did the gas cause problems?
3) How does a substance become a gas?
4) Why are gas particles difficult to control?

Answers

1) Methyl isocyanate.
2) It is highly toxic.
3) Heat a liquid until it evaporates.
4) They have high energy and so diffuse quickly.

Mark Inder

States of Matter – Changes of State

FREEZING AND MELTING

There was a documentary about water on TV, and Scarlett was watching it with Rob, her brother. 'We all know that things can exist as a solid, a liquid or a gas, but water is the only substance that occurs in all 3 states of matter naturally on Earth. There is liquid water in the rivers, lakes and oceans, ice in the polar and mountainous regions, and water vapour exists through volcanic vents as well as of course, clouds in the sky.'

'I wonder why that is,' said Rob. 'Easy silly,' replied Scarlett loftily, 'to become ice, water has to freeze, so the temperature of the water must decrease. That's why you only find ice and snow in cold places on Earth.

'To get steam, the water's temperature must increase. The liquid water then evaporates to become steam. Here's the thing though, a change of state is a reversible process, that's why when the kettle boils and all the steam hits the window, the water cools down straight away and becomes a liquid again – the change from gas to liquid's called condensation.'

Rob frowned, 'I'm not totally stupid you know, but I'll bet you don't know this – when a liquid becomes a solid its particles get closer together, but when a liquid becomes a gas it's particles move further apart.'

Scarlett threw a cushion at him. 'Look what you've made me do, I've been holding my chocolate bar, and the heat from my hand's melted it. It's virtually a milkshake!' 'That's not my fault, now please be quiet I'm watching this!'

Questions

1) How do you get solid water from liquid water?
2) What is the process called when a liquid becomes a gas?
3) What is condensation?
4) What happens to the particles of a substance when it solidifies?
5) What is the process of a substance turning from a solid to a liquid called?

Answers

1) You lower the temperature of the liquid water.
2) Evaporation.
3) When a gas turns into a liquid.
4) They get closer together until they are tightly packed.
5) Melting.

States of Matter – The Water Cycle

WATER MOVES AROUND THE EARTH

Jordan and Mohammed were visiting the local spring water factory in their summer holidays, and the tour guide was explaining about where the water comes from.

'You see, water is continuously recycled by the Earth in a process called the water cycle. Heat and wind evaporate the oceans, lakes, and rivers. The interesting thing about seawater when it evaporates is that it doesn't take the salt with it.

'The second stage of the water cycle is cooling of this water vapour, so it condenses to form clouds. There's a lot of water inside a cloud in vapour form, but later, the water particles start to stick to each other, meaning their mass increases. Eventually the weight of the water is too much for the cloud to hold, and so it falls out of the cloud. We know that as rain, but scientists call this third stage of the water cycle precipitation.

'Some of this rain just falls back directly into the water, but as we know, a lot of it hits the land – that's why umbrellas are so popular!' his smile died because he was expecting a laugh from his audience, but they were all examining some of the machinery in the building.

He coughed. 'Anyway, the final stage – called 'run off' is where the rain that's fallen on the land makes its way back to the ocean, and this can take thousands of years – and that's where we come in.'

Mohammed put his hand up. 'How do you collect all the water then, because if it hits the ground, doesn't it just make dirty puddles?' The guide seemed pleased that somebody in the group had asked him a question.

'This water has been travelling through the mountains around here for about 500 years, so the Earth has acted like a giant filter. When the water gets to the spring that this factory is built around, it's about as pure as you can get. Let's move on to the tasting room.'

Questions

1) What are the four stages of the water cycle called?
2) What factors affect the first stage?
3) How is rain formed?
4) What happens in the final stage of the water cycle?
5) How long can the water cycle take?

Answers

1) Evaporation, Condensation, Precipitation, Run-off.
2) The temperature and the wind speed.
3) Water particles clump together until they get too heavy for the cloud to hold.
4) All the water on the land eventually makes it way to a river, lake, sea, or ocean.
5) Thousands of years.

Mark Inder

Living Things and their Habitats – Classification

HOW WE GROUP ANIMALS

Sabina's class were visiting the Natural History Museum, and their guide was talking about classifying animals. 'It's relatively easy to classify animals and plants. For example, all mammals have fur or hair, and produce milk for their young.'

Sabina's hand shot up straight away. 'But dolphins are mammals aren't they, and they don't have hair – do they?' she claimed. 'Not true,' replied the guide matter-of-factly. 'Baby dolphins are born with a moustache that they lose a week or two after birth. But your point is well-made. Sometimes animals don't fit neatly into one classification.

'Everything with feathers you would think would be classed as a bird, but it's a fact that some dinosaurs such as velociraptor and T. Rex had feathers. If dinos were alive today, we might have some trouble separating them from the birds. Now, can anybody tell me the classes of animals?'

Sabina's hand rose again. 'Mammals and Birds!' she exclaimed. 'Good, but we've already had those,' said the guide. 'What else?' This time Jacob was first: 'Reptiles, Amphibians and Fish.'

'Excellent! – now all the animals we've mentioned have backbones, and we call those vertebrates. There is another class of animals that don't have backbones, these are the invertebrates.'

Sabina's hand rose for what seemed the hundredth time that afternoon. 'Aren't insects invertebrates miss?' 'Yes, they are Sabina well done!" the guide continued. When we classify a living thing, we ask questions that only have a yes/no answer. For example, does it have wings? If the answer is no, we know it's not a bird. This method of classification using questions with yes/no answers is called a classification key.'

Questions

1) Name the 5 classes of vertebrates.
2) How do you know an animal is a mammal?
3) What are animals without a backbone called?
4) Give an example of a class of invertebrate.
5) Name a method used to classify living things.

Answers

1) Mammals, Reptiles, Amphibians, Birds, Fish.
2) It gives birth to live young, it produces milk, fur on its body.
3) Invertebrates.
4) Insects.

Key Stage Two Science Comprehensions

Living Things and their Habitats – Extinction

PLATE TECTONICS

Uther and Lothar were looking at a giant map of the world at the Institute of Geology. 'Have you noticed how you could fit the right side of South America into the left side of Africa?' asked Uther. Lothar shrugged, 'I haven't, but now that you mention it, they do seem to fit together. Do you think they were together once?'

Uther was looking at another map. 'Look at this!' he exclaimed. 'It says that all the land was joined together in a super continent called Pangaea about 350 million years ago, but it started to break apart about 175 million years ago.'

'Wow, that's a long time!' observed Lothar. 'It says here that a lot of heat comes from the Earth's core – I think that's the middle of the Earth – and this heat rises and pushes the land around, so it takes ages for the map to change.'

'Yes,' said Uther, 'and the whole process is called Plate Tectonics. That's a cool word.' 'That's not the only thing that changes the Earth,' reported Lothar, 'Earthquakes and

Volcanoes can change everything as well, but that's not the coolest thing. It says here that an asteroid from outer space the size of Mount Everest smashed into the Earth 65 million years ago and it wiped all the dinos out!'

Uther continued: 'The explosion had the same power as 100 billion Hiroshima bombs – I don't know what that means, but it sounds powerful!' 'We better write this down for Miss otherwise we'll get into trouble!' ordered Lothar.

Questions

1) What is the innermost part of the Earth called?
2) How long ago did Pangaea exist?
3) What is the process called by which the Plates move?
4) How long can changes to the Earth take?
5) Name 3 things that can change the way the Earth looks.

Answers

1) The core.
2) 350 million years ago.
3) Plate Tectonics.
4) Millions of years.
5) Earthquakes, Volcanoes, Asteroids (Meteors).

Mark Inder

Sound – How Sounds are Made

SOUND STARTS WITH VIBRATION

Heidi and Ashley were doing their homework together in the library. Their teacher had asked the class to write an essay on how sounds start.

'Found it!' declared Ashley. She handed Heidi the physics book and pointed to a paragraph. 'Sounds start with the particle of a material vibrating,' she read. 'When an object is struck, the material moves from side to side, and we call this side-to-side motion a vibration. As soon as the object vibrates it makes a sound, and how fast the vibration occurs is called the frequency.

All sounds have frequencies. The higher the frequency, the squeakier the sound. Shorter, thinner objects will produce higher frequency sounds because it's easier to move them when they're struck so they vibrate more quickly than long, thicker objects.'

Heidi looked up. 'Have we got enough to do the essay?' 'Well, we can start it at least,' replied Ashley. She picked up her pen.

Questions

1) How do sounds start?
2) What do we call the side-to-side motion of an object?
3) What is frequency?
4) Squeaky sounds have what type of frequency?

Answers

1) Vibrations.
2) Oscillation.
3) How quickly a material vibrates.
4) High frequency

Mark Inder

Sound – How Sounds Travel

SOUND CAN GO THROUGH ANYTHING!

Eliza and Nathan were in the music shop to buy some speakers for their new apartment. 'That speaker vibrates,' observed Eliza, 'is that normal?' Jonathan, the shop worker, nodded. 'Sound starts with particles vibrating. Particles are the smallest part of a material.

The speaker, which is a solid, passes the vibrations onto air particles (which are a gas), and eventually those vibrations reach your ears, and you hear the sound.'

'So, sound passes through solids? I didn't know that.' admitted Nathan. 'They actually pass through solids much better than liquids or gases, because the particles are more rigidly packed in solids, so it's easier for the vibrations to pass from one particle to another.'

Eliza looked puzzled. 'You just said that sound goes through liquids as well. No way!' Jonathan thought for a moment. 'It's true, have you ever been underwater in the swimming pool? You can still hear everything that's going on above the water.

That proves that sound travels through liquids.' 'That's true, isn't it?' admitted Eliza.

Questions

1) What is a particle?
2) How do sounds start?
3) How do you know sounds travel through gases?
4) Why do sounds travel through solids much better than other states of matter?
5) How can you tell that sounds travel through a liquid?

Answers

1) The smallest part of a substance, such as an atom.
2) Particles vibrating.
3) Because we can hear sounds.
4) The particles in solids are closer together.
5) You can hear underwater, and ripples on water can be seen.

Mark Inder

Sound – Pitch

A NIGHT AT THE OPERA

Imran and Aisha were going to see the Opera La Boheme for the first time with their Dad.

'I hope this isn't going to be boring Dad,' Aisha said. 'Oh no,' said Dad, 'these people who will be singing have unbelievably powerful voices. Do you know, some singers can break glass with their voices?'

'Will we see that tonight, Dad?' exclaimed Imran excitedly. 'I doubt it, but I'll show you a video afterwards.' 'Cool!' said Imran, 'but how do they do that?' Dad thought for a moment. 'You know sound is vibration, yes?' Imran and Aisha nodded. 'When they sing a highly pitched note, like the way a whistle sounds, it makes the glass vibrate. If they sing a note that is high enough, the glass vibrates so much that eventually it breaks.

'Incredible really when you think about it.' Aisha looked puzzled. 'What do you mean by pitch?' Dad looked at Aisha, 'Vibrations have a frequency and that essentially means how quickly the vibrations of the sound occur. The higher the frequency, the higher the pitch. Squeaky sounds are high pitched, whereas the rumble of an Elephant is low pitched.

'You know when you're playing a recorder in school, and it has a load of holes in it?' 'Yes,' the two children said simultaneously. 'When you put your fingers over the holes, it shortens or lengthens the column of air inside the recorder, so the pitch of the sound changes. In other words, you play different notes.' 'I get it!' said Aisha as they all entered the theatre.

Questions

1) What is pitch?
2) Why can some singers break glass with their voices?
3) How is pitch related to frequency?
4) How does a recorder work?

Answers

1) The frequency of the sound.
2) They can make the glass vibrate so much that it breaks.
3) High frequency = High pitch and vice-versa.
4) The holes allow the player to change the length of the column of air running through the instrument, and by doing this it changes the pitch of the sound.

Key Stage Two Science Comprehensions

Sound – Volume

PROTECT YOUR EARS!

I had just got a job working on road maintenance with the local council, so I was attending a safety briefing. John, my boss, was heading the meeting.

'Now boys, some of the equipment you're going to be using is pretty loud. The jack hammers at their highest setting operates at a volume of 94 decibels, and even at the lowest setting they register 63 dB.

'In other words, when they work at higher energy, they are louder. Sustained exposure to that kind of volume could damage your hearing. All the vibrations made by the equipment is collected by your ears, so make sure you always wear your ear defenders when you're on site.

'If you need to speak to somebody, turn off the equipment first. Now, let's get to work!'

Questions

1) What is the unit of loudness?
2) What is the symbol for the unit of loudness?
3) What is the relationship between the energy used to make the sound and the loudness?
4) What does your ear do to the vibrations?
5) How can you protect your ears?

Answers

1) The decibel.
2) dB.
3) The higher the energy, the louder the sound.
4) It collects the vibrations.
5) Ear defenders.

Key Stage Two Science Comprehensions

Sounds – Sound and Distance

SOUNDS CAN TRAVEL FAR

Jonas and his Mum were watching a program about the animal sounds. 'The sounds animals make can travel huge distances,' said the narrator. 'They use their voices to attract a mate, or to warn competitors to stay away from their territory.

'For example, elephants can hear each other from up to 9 kilometres away and incredibly, elephants can hear sounds through their feet. Lion sounds can travel 7 kilometres. But the king of long- distance sounds are undoubtedly the whales such as the humpback, which can make sounds that can be heard by other whales across the ocean – 4000 kilometres! Their sounds travel so far when the whale makes very low frequency sounds which travel more easily through the water.'

'That's interesting isn't it, Jonas?' asked Mum. 'Mum, I'm trying to listen!' Jonas complained. The scene changed to a lab where the narrator was asking the scientist about sounds.

'The distance the sound can travel depends on the strength of the vibrations of the sound. The stronger the vibration, the further the sound will travel. But sound doesn't travel forever.

'Because the energy of these vibrations is dissipated in all directions, the further the sound goes from the source, the lower the energy becomes and eventually, no sound can be heard because there is no energy left to cause vibrations.' 'Okay Jonas you've seen enough. Time to do your homework.' 'Ah Mum!' said Jonas miserably.

Questions

1) What are animals trying to do when they make long-distance sounds?
2) How can whales make sounds heard across the ocean?
3) What factor does the distance a sound can travel depend on?
4) What is the relationship between distance and the strength of vibrations made by the sound?
5) Why doesn't sound travel forever?

Answers

1) Communicate with other animals.
2) The emit low frequency sounds.
3) The medium it is travelling through.
4) As the distance gets greater from the source, the vibrations decrease in strength.
5) Eventually the vibrations lose so much energy they dissipate.

Mark Inder

YEAR FIVE

Key Stage Two Science Comprehensions

Forces – Gravity

JUPITER WILL CRUSH YOU

Ju Fen was watching a sci-fi movie when her Dad walked in. 'What are you watching?' he said with interest.

'It's about this lady who was brought up on Earth but is in fact the queen of Jupiter. She's just found out about her heritage and now she's landed back on Jupiter.'

'Pah!' exclaimed her Dad, 'What a load of rubbish! You can't just walk around on Jupiter like you do on Earth.' Ju Fen paused the film. 'Why not?' she asked. Her Dad thought for a moment. 'Well, for one thing, the gravity would crush us humans like a bug. Jupiter, the planet with the biggest mass also has the biggest gravity – it's two and a half times that of Earth, so someone who weighs 100 kgs on Earth would feel like they weighed 250 kgs on Jupiter.

'Even the ship she came in on there would be squashed so it looked like a can of empty soda after the planet's finished with it!' 'Dad, what are you talking about?' Ju Fen's Dad tried to find the right explanation. 'Everything has mass, which we weigh in kilos right?' Ju Fen nodded, 'weight is different.

Weight is the effect of gravity on that mass. Wherever you are, your mass – in kilos remember – is the same, but your weight which is measured in Newtons is different depending on the planet you're on, or how close you are to the Sun.' 'Oh I get it!' interrupted Ju Fen, because the Sun has higher gravity, that would mean I would weigh more on it.' 'Good girl,' her Dad was pleased, 'So your bones wouldn't be built to stand all that weight. Like I said, you'd be crushed! To work out your weight, you take your mass and multiply by the gravity factor of the planet. On Earth It's 10, and on Jupiter it's 25. Interestingly, the Moon is only 1.6, that's why Neil Armstrong and the other people that landed on it had less weight and they could jump really far!'

Questions

1) What is gravity?
2) When mass increases, does gravity decrease?
3) What factor is different depending on where you are in the universe?
4) What is the unit of weight?
5) If the mass of somebody is 100kg, what is their weight on the Earth?

Answers

1) An attractive force.
2) The more massive an object, the more gravity it has.
3) Weight.
4) Newtons (N).
5) 1000 Newtons.

Mark Inder

Forces – Friction

FRICTION PRODUCES HEAT

'Miss, I'm freezing!' said Ruby. The class was on a nature walk in the local park in December.

'Where are your gloves Ruby?' asked Miss Stevens, 'you knew we were going to be outside today.' 'I left them at home Miss – sorry.' 'You don't need to be sorry to me, I'm not the one whose hands are cold!' Miss didn't seem to be very sympathetic.

'Rub your hands together, that'll get you warm.' 'How is that going to work Miss?' 'Remember our lesson on friction? Whenever you rub two things together, you get friction, and friction always produces heat. The harder you rub, the more heat you'll produce.'

Miss Stevens then raised her voice. 'Right class, some rules. There are some frozen puddles around here. The ice is smooth so there will be little friction between the ice and the soles of your shoes, so I don't want to see anybody sliding on ice while we're here in case you fall. Okay?' There was silence for a moment. 'Do you all understand?' 'Yes Miss!' replied thirty voices.

Questions

1) When does friction happen?
2) What is always produced by friction?
3) What happens when two surfaces slide against each other more forcefully?
4) Give an example of a smooth substance.

Answers

1) When two surfaces come into contact with each other.
2) Heat.
3) There is more friction.
4) Ice.

Mark Inder

Forces – Air Resistance

THE PARACHUTE JUMP

I was about to jump out of a perfectly good airplane from 3000 ft all for charity. I must confess my heart was pumping a bit but hopefully the instructor couldn't see any fear in my eyes. I adjusted the chin strap on my helmet nervously as I listened to the final instructions.

'Now remember!!!!' he shouted above the din of the engines. 'When you jump out, count slowly to 3 and check that you don't have any twists in your lines!' I swallowed. 'I remember.' I lied. 'Twists will make the canopy of the 'chute smaller, so you won't be able to build up the air resistance we need for you descend slowly enough to survive this!' And then he laughed.

'Thanks for reminding me! But you're not doing much to settle my nerves are you?' He smiled. 'These parachutes have a 100% safety record, they even make a version that's smaller, so you fall quite as quickly – lower air resistance you see, but they're for adrenaline lovers, not first timers, we'll get you one of those next time you come!' He grinned widely.

'There won't be a next time!' I promised. Suddenly, the engine noise reduced, and my jelly legs were dangling out of the plane. I wished I could go to the toilet. Then I heard 'Go!!!' and I jumped.

I counted and looked up – no twists, and the beautiful sight of the canopy filled my vision. All was peaceful, then suddenly, I laughed. 'This is fantastic!' I shouted to nobody at the top of my voice. I started talking to myself. 'So, the bigger the canopy, the more air particles it hits, the more air resistance there is and the more you slow down.' Just a short two minutes later I landed, and another came out to help me. 'That was fabulous, when can I do it again?!'

Questions

1) What do twists in the parachute do, and how does this affect air resistance?
2) What type of 'chute would you have if you wanted to fall more quickly?
3) What does air resistance do to objects?
4) How is the amount of air resistance related to the number of air particles?

Answers

1) They make the parachute smaller, so there is less air resistance.
2) A smaller 'chute.
3) It slows them down as it is a type of friction.
4) The more air particles an object comes into contact with, the greater the air resistance.

Key Stage Two Science Comprehensions

Forces – Water Resistance

BOAT SHAPES

'My family have been building boats for over 300 years, and the scientific advances in that time have seen incredible changes to the materials boats are made from,' said an old man. Jared and Natasha were on a canal boat holiday with their family, and they have stopped their boat for something to eat, and the man in questions just started talking to them.

'What do you mean sir?' said Jared politely. 'You can call me Arthur,' said the old man, who wore a seaman's cap and had a white beard. 'Boats were always made with wood in ancient times, and some still are, but many now are made of special kinds of plastics. I prefer boats to be made from wood myself.'

He thought for a moment. 'But the funny thing is that they all have the same basic shape, and they always have - even in ancient times. They are usually a bit pointed on the bow – that's the front you know.'

'Why is that Arthur? – I mean, why are they always pointy?' enquired Natasha. 'It makes 'em cut through the water more easily,' replied. 'There is this thing you see called water resistance. That's essentially the boat being slowed down by the amount of water it hits.

'The more water it hits, the higher its water resistance, and that means that it would be harder for the boat to sail, or row or whatever. Boats use fuel young missy, so if the water resistance is high, my fuel bill goes through the roof!'

Questions

1) What does water resistance do to boats?
2) Why do boats tend to have pointed fronts?
3) What would produce higher water resistance in boat design

Answers

1) It slows them down as it is a type of friction.
2) This shape cuts down the water resistance.
3) A flatter bow (front).

Key Stage Two Science Comprehensions

Forces – Simple Machines

BICYCLE GEARS

Libby and her Dad were on their first bike ride in the countryside, and they had just cycled up a steep hill.

'We'll stop here for a minute,' said Dad breathlessly. Libby Nodded, 'Before the hill, I was in a low gear and I was pedalling slowly, but when we got to the slope, I had to change up the gears and I was peddling really fast. Why is that?' wondered Libby.

Her Dad thought for a moment and then pointed to a big wheel with teeth in the middle of the bike underneath the seat. 'When you were on the flat, you were using this big cog here. That cog is difficult to move, so you pedal slowly but you generate more power. When you're on a steep slope, you must switch the gears to the smaller cog behind it. Because it's easier to move, you pedal more quickly but you will go more slowly because you don't generate the same power.'

'So, moving between the cogs increases or decreases power, depending on which cog you're starting with?' mused Libby.

'Exactly,' said Dad, pleased with her. 'Gears are simple machines we use in cars, drills – loads of things and like all simple machines, they help us increase a small force into a big one. In other words, they make the effort we put into something easier.'

Questions

1) What is a cog?
2) Which sized cog generated more power?
3) Which cog rotates more quickly?
4) What does switching gears do?
5) What is the effect of using a simple machine?

Answers

1) It is a wheel with teeth.
2) A larger cog.
3) A small cog.
4) It changes how easy it is to move the bike.
5) It reduces the effort needed to move a load.

Key Stage Two Science Comprehensions

Properties and Changes of Materials – Burning

YOU NEED THREE THINGS FOR A FIRE

The local fire service was visiting Danny and James' class, and the fireperson was talking about the conditions needed for fires to start. 'You need 3 things for fires to start,' she explained. 'Plenty of oxygen, which is in the air, a fuel, such as paper, wood, or gas like the fire in your living room. The last thing is heat. In science, we call those 3 things the fire triangle. Any questions?'

Danny put his hand up. 'What are flames miss?' She smiled. 'That's an excellent question! Flames are simply the hot gases that are produced when the fuel burns in oxygen. Fire is a chemical reaction that produces gases, usually carbon dioxide and water vapour. The carbon atoms emit light when they are hot, so flames always glow. The type of reaction is called an exothermic reaction, which means that heat is given out by the reaction.'

James raised his hand. 'What does the word combustion mean miss?' 'Another great question!' she laughed. 'It's simply the name scientists give to the process of burning a fuel in oxygen.'

Questions

1) What gas is in the air that's needed for fire to start?
2) Give 3 examples of fuels.
3) What gases are produced when fire happens?
4) Why does fire glow?
5) What does combustion mean?

Answers

1) Oxygen.
2) Paper, Petrol, Wood.
3) Carbon dioxide and water vapour.
4) Carbon atoms emit light.
5) Burning in oxygen.

Properties and Changes of Materials – Acid and Bicarbonate of Soda

HOW WE KNOW SOMETHING IS AN ACID

Ramani and Poppy were on an ecology fieldtrip with their biology teacher, Mr Mathers, who was talking to them about testing the water of the river and lake nearby.

'Remember what you've learned in school ladies. pH is the test of whether a substance is an acid, alkali or neutral.' 'Sir, we know! We were paying attention in class you know,' interrupted Ramani. 'Really?' He replied with disbelief. 'I seem to remember the two of you looking out the window at the time!'

They knew he was having fun with them; they were his best students. 'Okay then - Poppy, how are you going to test the water?' 'We are going to use the pH paper sir,' she explained. 'We take a sample of the water and then dip some of the paper in it.'

'Miracle of miracles!' said Mr Mathers with disbelief in his voice. 'Ramani, how are you going to know whether the water is acid or otherwise?' 'Easy sir, the paper will go different colours. Each colour represents its own pH on the pH scale. Neutral - which is green - is pH 7, anything under that is an acid, and anything over is an alkali.'

'Very good.' Mr Mathers said with a please gleam in his eye, 'but you didn't tell me the colours you'd see for acids or alkalis. Poppy?' 'Red for acids, and blue for alkalis. You'll have to ask harder questions than that to catch us out!'

Key Stage Two Science Comprehensions

Questions

1) What 3 things could the water be?
2) How is the liquid to be tested?
3) What is a possible pH reading of acids?
4) What colour will alkaline substances go?
5) What is pH 7?

Answers

1) Acid, alkali, neutral.
2) Using an indicator such as pH paper.
3) 0-6.9
4) Blue.
5) Neutral.

Mark Inder

Properties and Changes of Materials – Dissolving, Mixtures and Changes of State

SOLUTE + SOLVENT = SOLUTION

Brother and sister Mario and Kelly were watching their favourite science program on TV. 'Solutions are made up of 2 components,' said the presenter, 'the solute, which is typically a solid and the substance being dissolved, and the solvent – more often than not a liquid - and the substance doing the dissolving.

'The most common solvent is water, but there are others such as alcohol. The most common solution in the world is ocean water.' The presenter held up a jar with a clear liquid in it and then continued.' The main solute here is salt, and the solvent is water. There are also a few other solutes in there too.

'We can't see the salt because it is occupying the gaps between the water molecules and so appears to disappear when it dissolves.' The presenter paused for a moment before continuing:

'Solutions are types of mixtures. In chemistry, we can separate out the components of a mixture from each other by non-chemical means. In other words, the formation of mixtures is a reversible physical change as opposed to a chemical change where new substances are formed.'

Questions

1) What is the name of the substance being dissolved?
2) What does the solvent do?
3) Identify the solute in ocean water.
4) Why does the salt seem to disappear when it is dissolved in water?
5) Is the formation of a mixture a physical or chemical change?

Answers

1) The solute.
2) Dissolves the solute.
3) Salt.
4) It moves into the gaps between the water particles.
5) Physical change.

Key Stage Two Science Comprehensions

Properties and Changes of Materials - Filtering

THE COFFEE SHOP

Sadio had just got a job as a barista at the local outlet of a famous coffee company, and he was receiving training on how to operate the coffee makers. His boss, Virgil, was speaking.

'The machine first crushes the coffee grounds. Which is then put into the draw containing the coffee filters. Then close the drawer. The machine adds hot water, and the water dissolves the coffee that's inside the grounds. Because the coffee is soluble, it goes through little holes in the filter papers called pores. The left-over grounds are too large to go through these pores, so you will be left with the waste grounds in the filter.

'You must change the filters after every use because they can become damaged. If you make coffee with damaged filters, some of the grounds will end up in our customer's cups. We don't want that do we Sadio?' Sadio shook his head.

'Are there different filter papers for different types of coffee?' asked Sadio 'No,' laughed Virgil, 'this isn't a chemistry lab where they need filter papers with different sized pores!'

Questions

1) What is the solute when making coffee?
2) What are the holes in coffee filters called?
3) Why does the coffee go through these holes?
4) What is left in the coffee filters?
5) What happens if Sadio makes coffee with damaged filters?

Answers

1) The coffee powder.
2) Pores.
3) It is smaller than the pores.
4) Coffee grounds.
5) Some of the coffee grounds will end up in the liquid.

Mark Inder

Properties and Changes of Materials – Evaporation

TURNING LIQUID INTO GAS

Djibril was interviewing Dr Rupert Hynes for an article for the school magazine. Dr Hynes was a chemical engineer who worked for a pharmaceutical company. 'So, Dr Hynes, can you tell me what your job entails?' 'Well, I'm responsible for machines called evaporators. They are large, heated tanks that use evaporation to separate the medicines we make from the water that is used in the process.'

'Can you elaborate on that a bit more?' requested Djibril. 'Sure. What we make are pills that help people with heart conditions. We need the medicine to be dry so we can turn them into the pills, so we have to separate the water from the medicine before we can do that.'

Dr Hynes thought for a moment. 'You see, water is really useful in the process, because it has a low boiling point. That means we don't have to heat the tanks too much to make it evaporate. As you probably know from your science lessons, evaporation is the process of turning a liquid into a gas, in my case that would be water into steam. The heat gives the water the energy to turn from the liquid form into the gas form. Pipes lead the gas away from the tank and voila! We have only the medicine left.

'Evaporation is a brilliant way to separate soluble solids from liquids.' 'Thank you so much for your time, Dr Hynes,' said Djibril gratefully, that was very interesting!'

Questions

1) What is evaporation?
2) What type of energy is needed to evaporate liquids?
3) What type of solid is separated from the liquid?

Answers

1) When a liquid changes to a gas.
2) Thermal (heat) energy.
3) An insoluble one.

Mark Inder

Properties and Changes of Materials – Hardness

A VISIT TO THE BLACKSMITH

Elsa and Maisie were visiting a local blacksmith with the school so they could finish their history project on how swords were made in ancient times.

'Swords had to be hard,' the blacksmith said, 'but iron on its own was not hard enough to last, so ancient blacksmiths discovered that to make the hardest steel, they too iron and added charcoal, which is a form of carbon, and melted them together at about 1500 degrees.'

'Wow that's hot!' exclaimed Elsa. 'Yes, and I'm going to show you how that's done now, so don't stand too close to the furnace in case it spits out some hot material.'

He continued. 'First, we must heat the iron, so I am putting rods of iron into the furnace, after a few minutes, it will glow red hot. The colour tells us that the iron is just over 700°, so we need to heat it a bit more until it becomes white hot at 1200°. When that happens, we know it's time for us to add the carbon.

'While we're waiting for that to happen, let me explain something. What we are making here is called an alloy called carbon steel. Alloys are usually mixtures of metal that have different properties from the main metal.' He held up his left hand and presented a wide gold band on his ring finger.

'This is a gold wedding ring,' he said almost proudly, 'it's made of gold and silver, although it looks like it's made entirely of gold. Pure gold is a soft metal – not hard at all – and without the silver added, it would bend out of shape quickly. What we add to the main metal is called the 'additive', and additives change the properties of the metal.

'For example, stainless steel, which is used to make cutlery, is iron and chromium. Bronze is copper and tin, and brass is copper and zinc. The point is that materials are always made with their use in mind. There is an expression, 'about as much use as a chocolate teapot.' – think about why a teapot would not be fit for purpose if it was made from chocolate. Now we're ready to get back to making our carbon steel.'

Questions

1) Why do we need to make alloys?
2) What is an additive?
3) Give 2 examples of alloys and what they're made of.
4) What do we need to think of when we are making an alloy?
5) What do you think 'about as much use as a chocolate teapot' means?

Answers

1) They have different properties from their constituents, and therefore different uses.
2) Substances that are added to a metal to make an alloy.
3) Carbon steel which is iron and carbon, stainless steel which is iron and chromium, bronze is copper and tin, and brass is copper and zinc.
4) We should think about the use of the final material.
5) The chocolate would be an unsuitable material for a teapot as it would melt once hot water is added to it.

Key Stage Two Science Comprehensions

Properties and Changes of Materials – Transparency

SMART GLASS

I was looking to have some new windows installed in the office, so I was visiting a glass manufacturer to see what options there were.

'Here's the thing,' I said to Michael, the salesperson. 'I can't stand blinds or curtains, but my office window is south facing so sometimes I feel like an ant under a magnifying glass and the light becomes unbearable. What can you do for me?'

'We have the perfect thing for you,' replied Michael. 'This smart glass has 3 settings which you can control or set automatically to the external light levels. If it's dark, the glass automatically becomes fully transparent, so it lets all the light through. If it's getting a little bright outside, there is a setting to make the glass opaque which means the glass completely blocks the light. Finally, you can set the glass to translucent, so it only lets a certain amount of light through.'

'It sounds perfect,' I said, then a note of caution crept into my tone. 'How much does it cost?'

Questions

1) How would you classify a material that only lets some, but not all the light through?
2) What type of material do you need to block all the light?
3) Give an example of a transparent material.

Answers

1) Translucent.
2) An opaque material.
3) Glass, water.

Key Stage Two Science Comprehensions

Properties and Changes of Materials – Electrical Conductors

CONDUCTORS FOR SAFETY

A documentary on the history of electricity was on BBC 4. 'Many people died in house fires at the beginning of the 20th century. Electricity was just starting to gain a foothold in houses after the invention of the electrical light bulb. People were not exactly safety conscious.

'The best conductors are metals, and easily mined copper was used for the wiring in the walls, which often contained materials like paper as a packing material. The problem was, electrical wires become hot, and this heat in some cases was enough to ignite the packing material. Scientists realised that if they wrapped flexible electrical and thermal insulators around the wire, then safety would improve. They chose a substance called Indian rubber, a non-metal which had the just the properties builders needed.

'Since then, humans have invented many different types of plastic that are perfect for the task of insulating the copper wire. It is easy to make, and we can even colour-code the insulation.'

Questions

1) What type of substance conducts electricity well?
2) Give an example of a good conductor of electricity?
3) What type of substance is Indian rubber?

Answers

1) Metals.
2) Copper.
3) An insulator.

Key Stage Two Science Comprehensions

Space – the Solar System

SPACE DOCUMENTARY

Soothing music could be heard from the TV. A famous physicist was narrating a TV program on the formation of the solar system.

'5 billion years ago, the solar system had not yet formed,' he said in a calm, sober voice. 'There was simply a huge cloud of gas called a nebula. This cloud contained hydrogen, helium, nitrogen, iron, and silicon among other elements. This cloud was spinning, and as it did so, all the matter started to clump together.

'One of these clumps was particularly large, and as the matter became denser, it got hotter until eventually, all the matter ignited in a big ball of plasma. This plasma was our Sun, coming to life.'

'That must have been some explosion!' exclaimed Jack, who was watching the documentary with his brother Finn. The narrator continued, 'but the birth of our star was not the only thing happening in the nebula. Matter was coalescing in many other places, but there were eight other places where the matter was particularly dense. These eight places were to become the planets.'

The music suddenly changed to become more dramatic, and the narrator's voice went up a notch. 'The outer planets, Jupiter, Saturn, Uranus and Neptune, giant balls of gas, and the inner planets, Mercury, Venus, Earth and Mars, small balls of rock. One of these we call home – the Earth.

Key Stage Two Science Comprehensions

Questions

1) What was the name of the cloud the provided all the matter for our solar system?
2) Name some of the elements that made up this cloud.
3) How was the Sun formed?
4) What are the outer planets made of?
5) Name two inner planets.

Answers

1) A nebula.
2) Hydrogen, Helium, Nitrogen, Iron and Silicon.
3) A large part of the nebula got denser and hotter until eventually it ignited.
4) Gases.
5) Mercury, Venus, Earth, and Mars.

Mark Inder

Space – The Earth and the Moon

THE MOON ORBITS THE EARTH

Aisha and Bella were completing a project on the Moon and the Earth, so they were in the library. They were about halfway through but needed to find out about the orbit. Aisha was on the internet whilst Bella had her head in a book. 'Gotcha!' said Bella. 'What? Did you find it?' asked Aisha eagerly. Bella coughed as she recited one of the passages from the book.

'Like the way the planets orbit the Sun, the Moon orbits the Earth. Johannes Kepler and Isaac Newton explained why it's not a circle. It's because of the gravity of the Earth, it makes the Moon speed up as it gets closer to the Earth, and then slows down as it moves away – thus an elliptical path.' 'That's kind of like egg-shaped isn't it?' interrupted. 'Yes, but let me finish.' Replied Bella impatiently. Aisha rolled her eyes.

'It takes 28 days for the Moon to go around the Earth, and different parts of it are lit up as it goes around the Earth. The dark part is NOT the shadow of the Earth, it's the part that the Sun doesn't shine on.'

She looked up. 'The Moon doesn't shine you see, it's reflected sunlight' she explained. 'I know - that's the phases of the Moon!' exclaimed Aisha. Bella looked puzzled. 'Maybe we didn't need to come here seeing as you seem to know all about it.' She said sarcastically.

Questions

1) What is the shape of the orbit of the Moon around the Earth?
2) Why is the orbit not a circle?
3) How long does it take for the Moon to make one orbit?
4) Why are there phases of the Moon?
5) What is moonlight?

Answers

1) Elliptical.
2) Because of gravity.
3) 28 days.
4) Because of the relative positions of the sun, Earth, and Moon.
5) Sunlight reflecting off the Moon.

Animals including Humans – The Human Life Cycle

THE RIDDLE

In Sophocles' play Oedipus the King, a monster called the Sphinx was killing travellers on the road to Thebes who could not answer this riddle:

"What creature walks on four legs in the morning, two legs at noon, and three in the evening?"

Questions

1) What do you think the answer to the riddle is?
2) What stage of the human life cycle is represented in each part of the riddle and why?

Answers

1) Humans.
2) Baby, Adult, Old Person

Mark Inder

Living Things and their Habitats – Animal Life Cycles

NOT ALL MAMMALS GIVE BIRTH

Dr Bugstein from 'Creep and Slither' was in school, and he had brought with him various animals to show the children, so they were all gathered in the hall.

'This is the biggest Praying Mantis in the world, and one of the biggest insects. Her name is Esmeralda' He delightedly held up a huge insect that was crawling up his arm towards his face. The audience, including the teachers, gasped. He seemed totally unconcerned.

'This one's a Chinese Mantis which is strange because it's found in North America! Anyway, after the male and female have mated, she kills and eats him, so the Mantis babies benefit from all the nutrients in his body. She then lays about two hundred eggs which she hides in a safe place. But they don't have shells like the eggs that birds or most reptiles lay. Over 99% of insects lay eggs and they're quite slimy.'

Dr Bugstein then carefully placed the Mantis back in its tank and reached into another and brought out a beautiful light and dark brown snake. 'This beauty is called a boa constrictor, and like most animals, they have to mate to produce offspring.

'What's unusual about this reptile is that it gives birth to live young, like us humans and most other mammals. There are two mammals that lay eggs though, one of them being the duck-billed platypus. So, animals are either hatched from eggs, or grow inside their mother, who then gives birth to them.

'There's even an exception to this. Male seahorses carry their young until their birth.' He looked up with a smile. 'Now who wants to hold Cornelius here?' A hundred hands shot in the air and there was a big shout of 'Me!'

Questions

1) How do animals usually produce offspring?
2) How are the offspring of animals brought into the world?
3) How are mammals usually born?
4) Which types of animals usually lay eggs?
5) Which gender of animal usually gives birth to the young?

Answers

1) Sexual reproduction.
2) Live birth or hatching eggs.
3) Live.
4) Birds, fish, and some reptiles.
5) Female.

Living Things and their Habitats – Plant Reproduction

HOW PLANTS PRODUCE OFFSPRING

Gemma and Harrison were visiting the Royal Institution to attend the Christmas lecture on Reproduction of Plants and Animals. The lecture was to be given by world-renowned biologist, Professor Shirley Mendel.

'Reproduction is just the fancy science name for the process how species make copies of themselves. There are two types: asexual and sexual reproduction.' She paused for a moment. 'Asexual reproduction is where only 1 parent is needed. Plants and bacteria can reproduce asexually, and the offspring are exact copies of the parent.

'Sexual reproduction,' she explained, 'is where the organism needs two parents to produce offspring, which are not exact copies of the parent. One parent provides a sperm cell which fuses with an egg cell donated by the other parent. All animals produce offspring by sexual reproduction, but plants reproduce both ways!'

Questions

1) What is reproduction?
2) What are the two ways of reproduction in organisms?
3) What can plants do that animals can't regarding reproduction?
4) What happens in sexual reproduction?
5) What is the difference between the offspring produced asexually and sexually?

Answers

1) The process of a living thing making copies of itself (i.e., offspring).
2) Sexual and asexual reproduction.
3) Fertilise themselves.
4) Male and female sex cells fuse to eventually produce the offspring.
5) Asexually produced offspring are clones, whereas sexually produced offspring inherit characteristics of both mother and father.

Key Stage Two Science Comprehensions

YEAR SIX

Animals including Humans – The Heart and Circulatory System

THE CHECK UP

'Well doc,' said Mr Roth, 'how's my ticker?' The doctor smiled. 'Here's the angiogram – essentially an X-ray of your heart - and your heart looks pretty good.

'You can see here,' the doctor pointed, 'to the 2 small upper chambers of your heart. Each one is called an atrium – did you know atrium is the Latin word for room?' Mr Roth shook his head. The doctor coughed and continued. 'The two lower chambers here are called ventricles.'

'Wait a minute doc, something doesn't look right there. The side of my heart on the left seems to be thicker than the right. Is that anything to be worried about?' 'Not at all,' replied the doctor with an assuring tone, 'I'd be worried if they were the same thickness. You see, the heart is a muscle, and it's thicker on that side so that it can generate the power needed to pump the blood around your body.'

The doctor then used his pencil to trace a path on the angiogram. 'The heart leaves the heart through a major artery called the aorta, and a minute or so later the blood comes back, after having travelled 12 kilometres by the way, via a vein which is a different type of blood vessel to an artery - called the vena cava.' 'Very reassuring doc!' said Mr Roth approvingly.

Questions

1) How many chambers does your heart have?
2) What are the lower chambers called?
3) Why is the heart muscle thicker on the left-hand side?
4) Name the types of blood vessel.
5) What type of blood vessel carries blood away from the heart?

Answers

1) 4.
2) Ventricles.
3) This side needs to generate more power to pump blood around the whole body.
4) Arteries and Veins.
5) Arteries.

Key Stage Two Science Comprehensions

Animals including Humans – Diet

AN UNBALANCED DIET

The rules of the following film:

1) Morgan must eat McDonalds every day for breakfast, lunch, and dinner for one month.
2) He is not permitted to exercise in that time.
3) If the server asks him whether he wants to supersize his meal, he has to say 'yes.'

Watch:

https://www.youtube.com/watch?v=S9__23-zjhM&t=17s

Questions

1) Was Morgan healthy before this experiment?
2) How did the experiment affect Morgan physically?
3) Why do you think the food had this effect on his body?
4) What could Morgan do to regain his health?

Answers

1) Yes, he was physically fit and had a balanced diet.
2) Eating so much fast food poisoned his body.
3) It contained high amounts of unhealthy fats and sugars.
4) Stop eating fast food and return to eating a balanced diet.

Key Stage Two Science Comprehensions

Animals including Humans – Exercise

JOINING THE GYM

Matt and Josh had just joined the gym, and the rule was you had to get advice from a personal trainer before you started.

'Okay, so what do you want to achieve by being a member?' asked Sascha, the trainer. 'I want to get trim by losing fat around my waist,' replied Josh. 'What you want then, is a cardiovascular workout – or cardio for short. This involves running, cycling, and rowing. If you follow the cardio workout I give you 3 times a week for 6 weeks, you'll achieve your goal. Your body fat percentage will decrease, and you will see an improvement in heart and lung function.

'What about you Matt?' 'I want a bit more muscle than I have now.' Sascha thought for a moment. 'You'll spend your time doing resistance training. That consists of lifting weights, and different exercises target different muscles. Once again, you'll perform those exercises 3 times a week, and you'll be surprised at how quickly your muscle mass increases.'

Questions

1) What are the two types of exercise?
2) Which type of exercise would you perform if you want to increase your muscle mass?
3) How often do you need to exercise for it to have a positive effect on your body?
4) How does regular cardio affect your body?
5) Why do you need to do different exercises if you are lifting weights?

Answers

1) Cardiovascular and Resistance.
2) Resistance training.
3) Three times per week.
4) Decreases body fat and improves heart and lung function.
5) To target different muscle groups.

Key Stage Two Science Comprehensions

Animals including Humans – The Transport of Nutrients and Water

WATER AND THE KIDNEYS

Bethany and Maisie were attending a lecture in the local medical school, and Professor Winston Roberts, the world-renowned surgeon, was holding up something large, purple, and bean shaped.

'This,' he said in a deep voice, 'is the kidney of an ox.' He turned so all in the lecture theatre could see. 'All vertebrates have kidneys. They are responsible chiefly for filtering the blood, and the removing excess water that the body doesn't need through urination – peeing.' The audience laughed.

'Our bodies love water – we should all be drinking 8 glasses of water a day to keep us hydrated – but you will all know that when you drink lots of water in a short space of time, you'll be spending quite a bit of time going to the toilet.'

He grinned, 'that's your kidneys at work. Each kidney is like one million tiny sieves called nephrons working to removed unwanted substances from your blood. There are two.' He pointed to either side of the middle of his assistant's back, 'and the right kidney is slightly higher than the left. They work hard these two, filtering about 180 litres of blood a day. The average person urinates or pees 7 times a day, producing about 2 litres of urine.'

Questions

1) What is the role of the kidneys?
2) What do scientists call peeing?
3) How many glasses of water should you drink each day?
4) What are the tiny sieves in the kidneys called?
5) Where are the kidneys situated?

Answers

1) They filter the blood and removing excess water from the blood.
2) Urination.
3) 8 glasses per day.
4) Nephrons.
5) Middle of the back, on either side of the spine.

Key Stage Two Science Comprehensions

Electricity – Circuits

CELLS AND BATTERIES

'Why are batteries different Miss?' asked Harrison, who was trying to build a circuit with his lab partner, Holly.

'First, remember they're called cells in physics,' Miss reminded him, 'although two cells make a battery. Anyway, different devices have different voltage requirements, so different batteries are produced to have different voltages.'

Holly looked puzzled. 'What's voltage Miss?' Miss sighed. 'I already told you Holly, you must pay attention. Do you remember Harrison?'

Harrison smiled smugly. 'Of course I do Miss. Voltage is the energy that the battery gives to the circuit – it's like a push for the electricity.' 'Very good Harrison, 5 points for House Einstein!'

Harrison pumped his fist. Holly tried to redeem herself. 'And you get the amount of voltage in the circuit by just adding up all the voltage of the cells don't you Miss? And.... they make things like bulbs in the circuit brighter if you put more cells in.' 'Nicely done Holly, okay, 5 points for House Curie!'

Questions

1) In the real world, they're called batteries, what are they called in physics?
2) In physics, how many cells does it take to make a battery?
3) What is voltage?
4) How would you calculate the voltage in a circuit?
5) What could a higher voltage do to a bulb in a circuit?

Answers

1) Cells.
2) Two.
3) The energy that the battery gives to the circuit.
4) Add up the voltage of all the cells in the circuit.
5) Make it brighter.

Light – Reflection

A NIGHT TRIP ON A COUNTRY ROAD

'Dad, how do the little lights in the middle of the road know when to light up?' Dad had just picked me up from gymnastics, and because it was winter, it was pitch black on the country road we were driving on. Our path ahead was illuminated by little white lights down the centre of the road. He laughed.

'They're called cats eyes,' he said, 'and they don't light up because they can sense we are there little petal,' he said, 'they reflect the light from our headlights. Reflection means that light bounces off things, and we can see those things because that reflected light travels into our eyes.'

'Oh' I said, and then we both lapsed into silence as he concentrated on a series of tight bends as the road snaked around a series of high hills. But something was playing on my mind. 'Does everything reflect light then?' He thought for a moment. 'Oh no – some things give out their own light, like the Sun does, or a torch when it's on. Those things that produce their own light are described as luminous, whereas things that only reflect light are non-luminous. It's non-luminous objects that are reflectors.'

He paused while he went around a bend, then continued. 'The Moon isn't luminous, even though you would think it looking at it in the sky. It's simply a giant reflector of sunlight.' I think I'd started to piece a few things together. 'I think metals are good reflectors, because they're shiny, but black objects don't reflect the light well, because they're dull.' 'He looked over at me, pleased. 'Very good, but sometimes black things can be shiny too, and you can get dull metals – remember that.' 'Yes Dad.' I replied earnestly.

Questions

1) What do you think illuminated means?
2) When does reflection occur?
3) How do we see?
4) What property of objects makes a good reflector?

Answers

1) Lit up.
2) When light hits a reflective material.
3) The light is reflected into our eyes.
4) Shiny.

Mark Inder

Living Things and their Habitats - Microorganisms

TINY LIVING THINGS WE CAN'T SEE

'What does antibacterial mean Mum?' asked Katie, who was helping her Mum clean up the kitchen, and she was wiping the kitchen top with kind of wet tissue. Mum thought for a moment before answering.

'There are lots of tiny creatures so small that you need a microscope to see them,' she explained, 'and they are everywhere in numbers you can't imagine. We call them microorganisms, or microbes for short. The tissue is wet because it contains a fluid that kills a type of microorganism called bacteria. Some bacteria are harmful to humans, so we want the kitchen as free from bacteria as possible, because if they get onto our food, it can make us sick. That's why we're giving the tops a good wipe with these.'

Katie considered this as Mum carried on cleaning. 'The kitchen tops can make me sick?' she said with a worried frown. 'Don't worry it's only a precaution. There are other types of microbe too. Viruses, like the cold and the flu, and fungi, like yeast.' 'Yeast?' said Katie, 'don't we use that to make bread?' 'We sure do,' answered Mum, 'and that's the thing about microorganisms, some of them are good for us, and some of them are bad.'

Questions

1) What are microorganisms?
2) What is another name for them?
3) Name 3 types of microorganism?
4) What type of microbe is yeast?
5) Are all microorganisms bad for humans?

Answers

1) Living things so small you need a microscope to see them.
2) Microbes.
3) Bacteria, Fungi, Viruses.
4) Fungi.
5) No, some are beneficial.

Mark Inder

Living Things and their Habitats – Classification

DON'T USE HABITATS TO CLASSIFY ANIMALS

Gemma was in the Natural History Museum with her Mum. 'Can you believe this?' said her Mum, pointing to a glass case full of animals. 'What?' enquired Gemma, puzzled. 'This section is about classification, so to mix up the Mammals, Reptiles, Birds, Fish and Amphibians in one place is confusing.'

'Isn't this bit showing the Amazon habitat?' pointed out Gemma, but her Mum adamantly shook her head. 'The whole point of classification is to look at the features of an animal – the characteristics – and then group them together based on that. You wouldn't put a wolf with the reptiles, would you?'

Gemma shrugged. 'I don't see why not……' her Mum interrupted with irritation in her voice. 'Reptiles have scales, not fur, half of them lay eggs whereas a mammal gives birth to live young – they shouldn't be together,' she insisted.

Gemma's face took on a look of triumph, 'Actually I've just read over there that 2 mammals lay eggs, the platypus and the echidna.'

Mum looked half pleased and half annoyed at being corrected. 'True,' she admitted finally, 'there are always exceptions to rules, that's why scientists have to classify animals after considering more than one characteristic.' Gemma pointed to two men carrying a long sign reading 'The Amazon Habitat.' 'I told you so!' exclaimed Gemma triumphantly.

Questions

1) Name the 5 classes of animals.
2) Give an example of each.
3) What does the word 'characteristic' mean?
4) Which mammals don't give birth to live young?
5) Why do scientists have to consider multiple characteristics before classifying an animal?

Answers

1) Birds, Fish, Mammals, Reptiles, Amphibians.
2) Parrot, goldfish, dog, snake, frog etc.
3) Features of a living thing.
4) Platypus, Echidna.
5) Some animals in different groups have similar characteristics. For example, both bats and birds have wings.

Key Stage Two Science Comprehensions

Evolution and Inheritance - Adaptation

THE GIRAFFE'S NECK

Samira and Youssef were visiting the zoo with their Mum and Dad. 'Why does a giraffe have a long neck Mum?' Youssef asked. Samira interrupted before Mum could answer.

'Everybody knows that silly! It's so that they can reach the tops of trees for leaves to eat.' Youssef pulled his tongue at her. 'So, the tallest giraffes get to eat the most leaves because they can reach further.'

This time Mum spoke. 'Excellent logical thinking Youssef,' she said proudly, 'think about it for one second. If you can eat more, you're more likely to survive. That means that short-necked giraffes don't have as good a chance as long-necked ones, and what that means is that short-necked giraffes don't get to breed and pass on their long neck characteristic to their young. Over time, only giraffes with the long neck adaptation are born.'

Youssef looked puzzled. 'What does characteristic mean?' Samira poked fun at him again. 'You don't know anything do you?' Youssef frowned but ignored her while he waited for Mum to answer.

'You know how I've got brown eyes, but your Dad has green eyes?' Youssef nodded. 'Well, they're characteristics. It's essentially your physical features. All organisms have characteristics that are inherited from their parents that help them survive. Zebras have stripes because big cats only see in black and white, so it's difficult for a lion to see an individual zebra when it's in a herd – so stripes are an adaption that help them survive.'

Youssef. 'So, a chameleon is adapted to be able to change colour so it can camouflage itself?' 'Exactly,' confirmed Mum. 'Can we please go to the reptile house to see them?'

Questions

1) What does characteristic mean?
2) What does a long neck enable a giraffe to do?
3) Why are there no short-necked giraffes?
4) Where do animals get their characteristics?
5) Name a zebra adaption and how it helps them survive?

Answers

1) Features of living things.
2) Reach leaves at the top of trees.
3) They died out so could not pass on the long neck characteristic to offspring.
4) From their parents.
5) Black and white stripes.

Mark Inder

Evolution and Inheritance – Inheritance

__CHARACTERISTICS ARE PASSED ON__

It was our first family reunion for 3 years, and for the thousandth time since I'd known her, Aunt Betty said. 'You've got your Dad's eyes.' 'Yes, Auntie Betty.' I said, trying to sound polite.

'I think you've got his hair colour too, dear.' I think I wanted to shock her a little bit, so I said. 'Well, that's because my parents have each given me 50% of their DNA. Like you said, I have my Dad's eyes, ears, and hair colour.' I continued authoritatively, 'My Mum has given me her nose, mouth, and jaw line. My sister has Mum's blonde hair, and Dad's long nose, so when people have kids, although 50% of each parent's characteristics are passed on, it's a completely random mix so the kids might have different characteristics – that's why we look different from each other.

'Offspring are rarely identical to each other. It's called variation.' Aunt Betty's eyes were wide and her mouth a bit open in surprise. 'How old are you? You're a biological genius!' I flushed red, embarrassed at the praise. 'I'm 10

Aunty Betty, and I learned this in school a few months ago. I'm not a genius, I just remembered it that's all.'

'Nonsense,' exclaimed Aunt Betty, 'and never do yourself down dear. If you don't acknowledge your own talents, how can you expect anybody else to?'

Questions

1) What do you think characteristic means?
2) How much as a percentage of characteristics are passed on from each parent?
3) Name some characteristics can be inherited from parents?
4) Why are offspring not identical to each other?
5) What term do scientists give to the fact that offspring are not the same?

Answers

1) Features of a living thing.
2) 50% from each parent.
3) Eye colour, hair colour, height, hand size etc.
4) Characteristics are random.
5) Variation.

Key Stage Two Science Comprehensions

Evolution and Inheritance – Evolution

THE ADVANTAGE OF ADAPTATION

Professor Peter Salvak – or 'Paleo Pete' as he liked to be known, was being interviewed on TV.

'It's really very simple. Adaptations that are advantageous to a species get passed to subsequent generations, and disadvantageous ones die out. Eventually, most of the population of the species inherit that adaptation. Over time, and by that, I mean tens of thousands of years at least for animals and plants, a new species emerges which is the culmination of all the changes that have occurred that give the animal or plant an advantage in its environment.

'That process, we call evolution. Take human beings, the fossil record tells us that modern humans came into existence about 150,000 years ago, and we know from the record where they lived, what they ate, the size of their brains, how tall and strong they were and how old they lived to. We have not actually changed that much from that time. Amazing really when you think where we've come from to walking on the Moon. Anyway, humans haven't really needed to evolve because we rule our environment to a certain extent, and some believe that our evolution has ended because we don't need new adaptions. I don't by the way!'

Questions

1) How does evolution of a species occur?
2) What can the fossil record tell us about human evolution?
3) Why do some scientists believe that human evolution has stopped?

Answers

1) Advantageous adaptations are passed on through the generations until all the individuals in a species have them.
2) How long-ago species appeared, what species ate, what their environment was like etc.
3) We control our environment.

WOULD YOU LIKE ACCESS TO A SCIENCE SCHEME THAT HAS EVERYTHING YOU NEED TO TEACH OUTSTANDING PRACTICAL SCIENCE, INCLUDING 500 ACTIVITIES AND 120 TEACHER TRAINING VIDEOS?

GET A FREE MONTH OF UNRESTRICTED ACCESS TO EVERYTHING!

Please visit www.pzaz.online for further details.

Thank you so much for buying and reading this book.

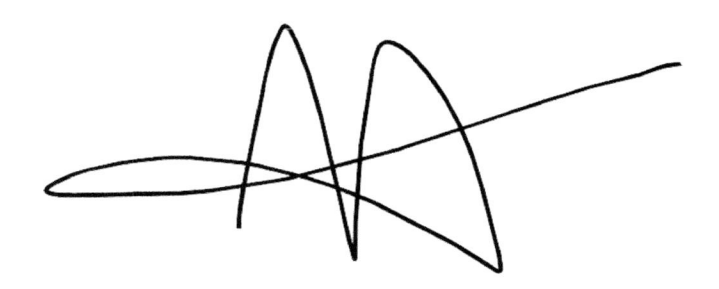

Printed in Great Britain
by Amazon